Chapter 1
Introduction: What *Is* Burnout, Anyway?

In the late 1960s, industrial/organizational psychologists expressed concern about high-achieving, rapidly rising young executives who deteriorated into victims of chronic fatigue and who demonstrated drastic attitude changes, decreased performance, and occasionally "office paranoia" (French and Caplan, 1972; Kermish and Kushin, 1969; Podell, 1967; Weinberger, 1970). These suffering individuals were frequently labeled "flame outs" in an attempt to semantically describe the loss of their initial thrust as resembling a rocket blast that ran out of fuel (Patrick, 1984b). The term "burnout" first appeared in the literature when Freudenberger (1974) used it in a journal article describing the suffering of helping professionals who appeared to wear out in their roles after several years of service. Other early works on the subject of burnout used terminology such as "bureaucratic blahs" (Pearse and Peizer, 1975), "occupational tedium," "career fatigue," and "professional stagnation" (Vessell, 1980), as well as "goldbricking" (Argyris, 1957), "work rebelliousness" (Litweis and Stringer, 1968), and "occupational distress" (Justice and Justice, 1981) to describe what Maslach later identified empirically as the burnout phenomenon. (Maslach, 1982; Maslach/Pines, 1977 and 1979).

Today, the word burnout has become very common in popular usage. A student who has been working on a term paper for five hours may describe feeling "burned out" yet have plenty of immediate energy available for a new, perhaps social, activity. Similarly, library instructors may describe themselves as burned out on bibliographic instruction after several years of freshman classes but become quickly enthused about preparing a new seminar on computer-assisted instruction for colleagues. Public, school, academic, or special librarians who become apathetic and cynical about certain aspects of their jobs may claim to be burned out on librarianship, only to be refreshed by a new project, different responsibilities, or environmental changes. Under current usage, burnout has been used as a synonym for words with very different meanings, such as "alienated," "indifferent," "apathetic," "cynical," "discouraged," or "depressed" (Brill, 1984). In work environments, it is generally used to describe a regression of the individual to a minimal level of organizational and professional performance and growth.

Although the term burnout is most often applied to people in various helping professions, such as mental health workers, and clergy, a wide variety of other professionals have also recognized the phenomenon as applicable to their own work. These include attorneys (Maslach and Jackson, 1978), health care professionals (Fox, 1980; Gray-Toft, 1980; Patrick, 1979), recreation therapists (Vessell, 1980), music therapists (Bitcon, 1981), police officers (Maslach and Jackson, 1979), educators (Hendrickson, 1979; Reed, 1979; Walsh, 1979), and many others (Cherniss, 1980). In 1981, *Time* magazine published an editorial noting that the concept of burnout has been applied so broadly that it seems to be used to account for *any* deviation from job satisfaction, enthusiasm, commitment, idealism, or ebullience and could be labeled as the syndrome of "the burnout of almost everybody" (Morrow, 1981). Christina Maslach, considered by many to be the primary pioneer of empirical research on burnout, became interested in the concept in the early 1970s. This is her description of the immediate and immense impact of her earliest work:

> I tried out my initial ideas at a national convention in 1973. I then developed a working concept of the burnout process, which I described in *Human Behavior* magazine in 1976. The public response to this article was overwhelming. Thousands of letters and telephone calls poured in from all parts of the United States and Canada. People wanted more information about burnout, some asked for help with their specific difficulties, and some expressed relief that at last this taboo topic had been made public. The article was reprinted or abstracted in many newspapers, magazines, and books; circulated widely in dozens of professional newsletters; assigned as required reading for various training and in-service programs; and distributed as a special handout at workshops and conventions. Clearly, burnout was a major concern for many people; it was as if a raw nerve had been touched. (Maslach, 1982, pp. 7–8).

So far, more than fifteen definitions of burnout have been identified in the social psychological literature, and several sets of stages have been theorized for the phenomenon (Dworkin, 1987). In less than a decade after Maslach introduced the idea, over 1,000 journal articles and nearly 100 books were written on the subject (Maher, 1983).

DEFINITIONS AND THEORETICAL CONSIDERATIONS

Common dictionary definitions of burnout include both noun and verb forms. As a noun, it is defined as "exhaustion of physical or emotional strength" (*Webster's Ninth New Collegiate,* 1987). The verb form is even more descriptive: to destroy, obliterate, or to cause to fail, wear out, or become exhausted by making excessive demands on energy, strength, or resources (*Webster's Third,* 1976). An excellent historical review of the word burnout from an early recorded occurrence in 1710 to the present can be found in a scholarly paper by Watstein (1979); it will not be summarized here but is highly recommended for those who enjoy lexicographic research.

Freudenberger's (1974) early definition of burnout wasn't really a definition at all; it consisted of a collection of behavioral traits that were observed in members of the helping professions who were pursuing impossible goals under impossible conditions. These traits included cynicism, negativism, inflexibility, rigid thinking, unhappiness, boredom, and psychosomatic illnesses—an unenviable list to say the least. Freudenberger suggested that the unrelenting pursuit of impossible goals with insufficient resources resulted in the transformation of committed, caring professionals into exhausted, uncaring drones. The most frequently given definition of burnout is the one used by Christina Maslach and Ayala Pines, who identified the burnout syndrome as a multifaceted state of emotional, physical, and mental exhaustion caused by the chronic stress that occurs when members of the helping professions experience long-term involvement with other people in emotionally demanding situations. In a variety of empirical studies, they found burnout to be highly correlated with staff turnover, employee tardiness, individual intention to leave a job, health problems, use of alcohol, an increased sense of hopelessness, and loss of idealism about work. They also found evidence that burnout is negatively correlated (that is, burnout is high when the other variables are low) with work satisfaction, high self-esteem, and general satisfaction with one's life (Etzion and Pines, 1981; Maslach and Pines, 1977, 1979; Pines, 1981a, 1981b, 1982; Pines and Aronson, 1980, 1981; Pines, Aronson, and Kafry, 1981; Pines and Kanner, 1982; Pines and Maslach, 1978, 1980).

One theory used to explain the burnout phenomenon is that inner resources can be depleted. Many authors equate burnout with the physical process of fuel consumption, with eventual depletion through burning. The idea is that people house a finite reservoir of personal energy, which can be used up if not appropriately replenished. Here is Potter's (1980) illustration of this depletion process:

> Like fire, motivation gets stronger and burns hotter or diminishes and burns out. There is no constant state. But even the hottest fires will burn out, so we tend them, fanning and stoking them, occasionally adding another log. Like fires, people are not static. When motivation wanes, we burn out. Yet there is no need for alarm as long as we have fuel and we know how to tend motivation and we haven't waited too long. (p. 1)

Muldary (1983), provides an articulate and colorful version of the same idea:

> It is common sense to conclude that someone who "burns out" must have been "on fire" at some time. In this connection the term was once used as a loose psychiatric label for psychopaths whose chronically antisocial behavior seemed to die out after the age of forty. It was also used, and still is in some contexts, as a street label for people who appear to be emotionally amd mentally disorganized because of chronic drug use. (p. 2)

To understand the concept of burnout, it is vital to have a good understanding of the concept of stress. Stress can perhaps best be defined as an individual's emotional, physical, and behavioral responses to life's demands. These demands, which are of an infinite variety, are the stressors to which humans respond in their experience of stress. The notion of stress as a part of living is so commonplace now that it's hard to imagine that the idea was undeveloped and the term was essentially unknown until 1936, when Hans Selye first reported on his investigations in this area.

Selye's General Adaptation Syndrome

Selye's recollection of the earliest beginnings of his theory dates to 1926, when he was a nineteen-year-old medical student at the University of Prague. A well-respected professor presented five patients suffering from different ailments and challenged the students to diagnose them. Selye, like his peers, noted the differences among the patients' symptoms and worked at trying to guess their cause. However, unlike his classmates, Selye also observed similarities among the five patients and found himself considering these as well. All five patients seemed to be depleted of energy and were listless, haggard, and withdrawn. After thinking it over that evening, Selye approached his professor the next day, seeking permission to investigate what he loosely described as the "syndrome of just being sick." As Selye recollected in an interview with Laurence Cherry (1978), "the most humiliating conversation of my life ensued" (p. 64). Selye was promptly advised to leave such theorizing to more experienced scientists. Fortunately, Selye didn't. He graduated first in his medical school class, went on to get a second doctorate in organic chemistry, obtained a Rockefeller Research Fellowship, and eventually settled at McGill University in Montreal, where he published his theory of human stress. During the next forty years, he reported the results of his lifelong investigations of the General Adaptation Syndrome in over 1,600 journal articles and thirty books.

According to Selye's theory, a three-stage reaction occurs in all stress and these three stages make up the General Adaptation Syndrome. In Stage 1, called the Alarm Stage, the body recognizes a stressor and immediately prepares for flight or fight. Various endocrine glands are stimulated to release hormones that cause an increase in heart rate and respiration, an elevation of blood sugar, increased perspiration, dilated pupils, and slowed digestion. A burst of energy is thus physiologically readied, and one can choose to use it to fight off the stressor or flee from it. Stage 2, the Resistance Stage, occurs if the stressor is conquered or escapes. If the stressor is gone, the body repairs itself by allowing hormone levels to return to normal, which allows decreasing heart rate and respiration, lowering of blood sugar, decreased perspiration, normal pupillary response, and a normal rate of digestion. If the stressor is not gone, however, the body stays alert. When the body must stay alert, at Alarm Stage levels, for a long period of time, Stage 3, the Exhaustion Stage, is eventually reached. In the Exhaustion Stage, the body experiences the various diseases of stress such as heart arrythmias or headaches. If the Exhaustion Stage is not relieved, eventually death results.

Selye did not view all stress as bad, however, and defined it as having two sides, one positive and one negative. In positive stress, or eustress, the stressors promote well-being by serving as catalysts and stimulants to push the individual toward achieving at a high level. Selye believed that many people, those whom he calls "racehorses," literally thrive on high levels of stress. However, the downside of this idea is that some stress is harmful. Continuous stress over a long period is quite harmful and worthy of the name Selye applied to it: distress.

Zastrow (1984) suggests that the most useful definition of burnout is one that describes it as a reaction to extremely high levels of stress, with stress meaning the emotional and physiological reactions humans make when faced with stressors of infinite varieties. From this perspective, the Exhaustion Stage of Selye's (1936) classic stress theory can be viewed as the definitive description of burnout. Remember, the Exhaustion Stage is reached after high levels of stress have been encountered for an extended period of time; in the Exhaustion Stage the body begins to break down physically until eventually death occurs.

Burnout as Work-Related Stress

A number of authors (Edelwich and Brodsky, 1980; Melendez and Guzman, 1983; Veninga and Spradley, 1981) note that burnout is not simply the result of long periods of high levels of stress; rather, it is a specific response to unrelieved *work-related* stress. As a viable definition, the idea that burnout is related to workplace stressors can be explained by the idea that burnout is a stress-related malady with primary roots in the setting where people invest the majority of their time and energy. For most professionals, this setting is the work environment (Tubesing and Tubesing, 1982). Veninga (1979) describes burnout a little more behaviorally, but with the same intense focus on work. He says burnout is "a debilitating psychological condition brought about by work-related frustrations that result in lowered productivity and morale" (p. 45).

Emotional, Physical, and Mental Exhaustion

Nearly all of the current research studies on burnout characterize it as a syndrome with three major types of exhaustion: emotional, physical, and mental. All three types of symptoms must be present in response to work-related stressors in order for the burnout process to be considered present.

Emotional Exhaustion

Emotional exhaustion, which Maslach (1982) characterizes as the heart of the burnout syndrome, occurs when a person becomes overly involved emotionally, begins to overextend personal resources, and feels overwhelmed by the emotional demands of other people. Within the burnout syndrome, emotional exhaustion may be represented by feelings of apathy, helplessness, hopelessness, emptiness, chronic dissatisfaction, and cynicism, along with a sense of powerlessness or entrapment (Muldary, 1983).

Physical Exhaustion

The emotional exhaustion of burnout is frequently accompanied by physical exhaustion. The burnout victim may report feeling tired and run down all the time, having difficulty getting up for work in the morning, or having trouble sleeping at night. The steady experience of increased tension that is an integral part of emotional exhaustion inevitably affects physical well-being, resulting in a sense of depletion, of energy drain without replenishment. The end result of emotional exhaustion is a feeling of being drained and used up, lacking the physical energy to face one more person or one more day. According to Pines and Aronson (1988), most people experience burnout as a gradual erosion of their personal energy, and the physical exhaustion of burnout is never divorced from the mental and emotional exhaustion that accompanies it. For example, a physically exhausted runner completing a marathon run is not burnt out because the emotional state accompanying the feat is exhilaration rather than emotional depletion. A burnout victim who is equally physically exhausted has no accompanying exhilaration to counterbalance distress with eustress.

Mental Exhaustion

Emotional distress also has a significant effect on cognitive abilities, and persons experiencing the emotional exhaustion of burnout are likely to notice reduced abilities in the areas of attention and concentration skills, problem-solving skills, judgment, or memory. These are not true cognitive deficits; rather, they are emotionally generated disruptions of cognitive processes that reduce the effectiveness of the individual's actual capacities. A concomitant loss of self-esteem and a significant decrease in one's sense of personal accomplishment may occur as well. Pines and Aronson (1988) note that mental exhaustion is usually characterized by the development of negative self-attitudes about one's value, work, and life itself. Burnout victims report feeling inadequate, inferior, and incompetent. In addition, they begin to experience negative feelings toward others, especially those with whom they come in contact most frequently.

> The painful disillusionment with work as an avenue for finding meaning in life is at the core of the negative attitude change and mental exhaustion of burnout. When people are unable to derive a sense of significance from their work they experience feelings of personal failure and negative attitude change toward themselves (for not being good enough, strong enough, or knowledgeable enough to get the job done), toward their clients (who were supposed to provide that sense of significance by improving, learning, or healing), and toward colleagues (who might have helped by providing support and challenge, but did not). (Pines and Aronson, 1988, pp. 15–16)

Once emotional, physical, and mental exhaustion are being experienced, the downward spiral toward total exhaustion begins to seem overwhelming and inevitable.

PRACTICAL CONSIDERATIONS

The variety of possible responses to job stress is of great magnitude and has been reported frequently in personnel and psychology journals. The result of the emotional, physical, and mental exhaustion of burnout is a full syndrome of symptoms ranging from relatively mild to quite severe, even life-threatening. Burnout victims have reported that job stresses they may have recognized in the past suddenly begin to feel overwhelming, so overwhelming that the discouraged professional finds it increasingly difficult to respond to the everyday demands of work. Eventually, total overload occurs, and the frustrated worker essentially shuts down in defense against the burden of overload. The result is apathy born of frustration. Behavioral withdrawal in a variety of forms often is evident: burned-out librarians may spend more time away from others in isolated locations, absenteeism increases, procrastination on the job increases, and indifference replaces enthusiasm. For many burnout victims, a renewed desire for work to be meaningful is once again aroused, in hope that a renewed sense of meaningfulness might resolve the situation. Unfortunately, this hope is seldom realized.

Frequently, personal demands also seem intolerable, as the burnout victims have no energy available to deal with family or friends who seek pleasurable, interesting, and dynamic relationships with them. As concentration becomes more difficult, even the completion of routine tasks deteriorates and previously well-organized high achievers may have trouble paying their bills on time or getting their laundry done. Of course, many physical ailments are experienced as well, so headaches, respiratory problems (such as coughs that hang on for months), vague indispositions, increased susceptibility to colds and flus, and mild cardiovascular problems begin to surface. Without alleviation of the chronic triggering stresses, burnout victims can become permanently debilitated by the phenomenon and may literally be unable to continue to work. Although their skills remain intact, their ability to use learned skills is drained (Potter, 1980).

SUMMARY

It is probably quite evident by now that burnout is more than a simple malaise or indisposition, more than an episode or two of extremely high stress. Rather, it is a syndrome of advanced and wholistic responses to extended periods of high levels of stress that results in a variety of emotional, physical, and cognitive symptoms. These symptoms are so disrupting and distressing that they appear totally overwhelming to the individual.

The various definitions offered by researchers in mental health and other fields allow some generalizations despite their variance in semantics, philosophies, and underlying theories. First, burnout is not synonymous with job stress, although job stress is a primary factor in the burnout process; burnout is a response to long unrelieved (and cumulative) periods of high levels of work-related stress. Second, burnout manifests itself as a combination of emotional, physical, and mental exhaustion that is expressed in attitude and behavioral changes felt by the individual victims and observed by those around them. Third, individuals who work in helping professions may be at higher risk for burnout. Fourth, the primary salient feature of work-related burnout is the disruption of a previously satisfactory relationship between individual professionals and their work environments or careers.

Given these generalizations, it is easy to visualize librarians as potential victims of the process by which once committed professionals become ineffective in managing daily work stresses in a helping context, become exhausted, and, as a result, disengage from patrons, colleagues, and library work.

However, it is impossible to work efficiently without generating some degree of stress, and some research studies have shown that a stress-free life is in itself stressful. The trick is to manage stress so that a positive balance between productive stimulation and overwhelming distress can be maintained. Burnout is not an abrupt, overnight phenomenon. Rather, as Selye's studies on stress indicate, it is a cumulative process of increasing stress levels without appropriate reductions after initial alarms. If individuals become aware of the potential generators of burnout, learn to self-monitor early signs of increasing stress, and practice a variety of stress management techniques, burnout can be prevented. If the process is already under way, individuals can be encouraged to view it as a trigger for personal growth, a crisis that presents an opportunity to learn effective means to reverse it. The prevention and, if necessary, the reversal of burnout are the primary focus of this book. The remaining chapters are largely devoted to presenting practical information on the recognition of stress and the prevention of burnout.

Chapter 2
What Causes Burnout?

The earliest literature on the burnout phenomenon suggests a clear causative connection between continuously high levels of stress in the work environment and individual burnout. The earlier research on work-related stress, however, suggests that the causes of stress are found within the person as well as the work environment (Beehr and Newman, 1978), and both potential sources have been investigated by researchers exploring the burnout phenomenon in the 1980s. According to Pines and Aronson (1988), the timing, manifestations, and consequences of burnout depend both on the individual and on the work environment. Some people burn out faster than others, and some occupations promote burnout at a faster rate than others. At the present time, we still know more about environmental stressors that contribute to burnout than we know about personal characteristics that may be conducive to increasing one's burnout potential, but data on the latter are increasing. Most burnout victims assume that the fault lies in themselves rather than in their stars or their work environment. Even though they may recognize the stresses inherent in the environment, they think they should be able to handle the situation. Because burnout is the result of chronic everyday stress rather than the result of occasional crises, what changes over time is an individual's tolerance for the constant stress. Unfortunately, most people see decreasing stress tolerance as personal failure. Rather than attributing their growing discomfort and distress to some unknown cause like a burnout process or to the chronic nature of the stresses they encounter at work, they accurately observe that the stress of the job has remained fairly constant and thus reason that they are deficient in some way or incompetent. Essentially, burnout victims tell themselves, "This has always been a stressful job, but I'm just starting to have troubles now, so there must be something wrong with me." Both the work environment and personal characteristics play a very significant role in the etiology of burnout and are worthy of comprehensive review.

CAUSES IN THE WORK ENVIRONMENT

Some very specific aspects of the work environment are highly correlated with burnout. These include the amount of professional autonomy allowed within the organization and the proportion of time spent dealing with the public. Role conflict and role ambiguity are also significant variables. Opportunities for personal accomplishment and positive feedback for accomplishments also have a specific relationship to the development of burnout. An additional factor is how much impact professionals feel they have on the system in which they work. No-win situations, continuously heavy workloads, and stressors in the physical environment are also important. In this section, each of these contributing factors will be explored separately.

Lack of Professional Autonomy

In a survey of corporate managers, Pines and Aronson (1988) sought to discover executive views of the hopes and expectations most often held by people entering a professional career. They also wanted to know what the executives considered to be the primary stressors encountered in professional work. Ranked high among the hopes and expectations reported by the executives was a strong desire for autonomy, the opportunity "to be able to do my own thing, express myself" (p. 58). A primary stressor was "administrative and bureaucratic interference" (p. 58). Other investigators have also found that new professionals prize autonomy and consider its absence or relative lack a major stressor (Perlman and Hartman, 1982; Richardson and West, 1982; Rosenthal et al., 1983). Maslach (1982) notes that burnout is particularly high when professionals lack a sense of personal control over the service they are providing. This lack of control can range from being told exactly what to do and how to do it, to having no input into policy or decision making. People not only experience frustration and anger in these types of situations, but they may also feel ineffective and perceive themselves as failures. Library professionals work in highly complex organizations that are frequently intolerant of professional autonomy, and some librarians may find this a factor in their own personal stress levels.

Dealing with the Public

Work that involves social interaction with people can be very tiring. It requires a lot of energy to be patient in the face of another's frustration, to be active in clarifying unclear requests and expectations, and to demonstrate appropriate social skills no matter what one's actual feelings. The special rules that govern the helping relationship dictate what is expected from the provider and from the recipient (Maslach, 1982). In a library, the provider is expected to be appropriately calm when faced with frustrated users or angry patrons. The etiquette of librarianship requires librarians to express gratitude for gift acquisitions (even the fiftieth copy of last year's *National Geographic* magazine), to patiently explain the *Reader's Guide* innumerable times, and to remain calm and effective when faced with five high-priority and complex information requests in a single half hour or when required to explain the library's acquisitions policies to angry parents who disapprove of the material their children checked out. Some of the rules are explicit, in the form of written guidelines or policies generated by the library administration. Others are implicit, the unstated guidelines of social norms and power relationships learned in library school and through general life experience. Explicitly, librarians are likely to be required to respond to all patrons in a courteous and informative manner. Implicitly, they are likely to be required to demonstrate kindness, patience, caring, and respect, and to suppress anger, frustration, and impatience. They are supposed to uphold the rules without being tyrannical. They are supposed to answer questions speedily, efficiently, and comprehensively. Above all, they are supposed to be *helpful,* guiding users through the complex maze of information retrieval. As Maslach points out, the implicit rules can be so constraining that they contribute to an individual's stress and subsequent potential for burnout.

Working with the public also means working with other professionals outside of your own organization. Kahn and his associates (1964) identify three particular performance factors that are likely to increase stress on the individual working within an organization. The first is the necessity to make frequent contacts beyond the boundaries of the individual's department within the organization, the second is high demand for contact beyond the boundaries of the organization, and the third is high demand for innovative and creative problem solving. In the past, librarians might have thought immediately of reference staff as the most likely to be affected by these three factors, as they are all clearly inherent in reference work. However, with the sophistication and complexity of technical services for information organization as well as the tremendous complexity of the types of information all librarians deal with on a daily basis, it is clear that these factors have become integral parts of all types of information work. Today, librarians perform significant numbers of interlibrary transactions and provide other document delivery services; use automated systems for acquisitions, cataloging, and documents and serials control; and engage in multiple library cooperative efforts. Thus, in addition to the need to deal directly with the nonlibrarian public in social interaction, librarians carry the additional burdens of frequent interaction with their library peers both near and far. If dealing with the public is a factor in burnout, librarians are undoubtedly at risk.

Role Conflicts

Two significant types of role conflict have been shown to promote burnout. One is a lack of fit between individuals and the job, and the other is a conflict between the individual's values and the demands of the job (Daniels, 1985; Justice, Gold, and Klein, 1981; Mueller, 1979; Rosenthal et al., 1983). Both situations result in significant personal discomfort and increased stress that further tax the individual's ability to function effectively without potential exhaustion of personal resources.

Other types of role conflicts may also become significant chronic stressors in the workplace. Role conflict can be experienced when one works for more than one supervisor, particularly if the demands the different supervisors make on the individual appear to be incompatible (Visotsky and Cramer, 1982) or present conflicting priorities. The recent move toward job sharing may also generate role conflict if the individuals sharing the job have different goals, philosophies, or expectations. Another type of role conflicts is that between job and personal expectations, as in the case of working parents who must balance parenthood responsibilities with the demands of their careers (Potter, 1980).

Temporary role conflict exists in situations that require a professional to suppress personal feelings in order to meet job expectations. Librarians, for example, are expected to respond to obnoxious patrons with patience and tact rather than with a snarl. This type of temporary conflict is a universal experience, and most people have little difficulty with occasional situations in which they must briefly suppress feelings. However, excessive control of the expression of feelings is counterproductive and has been correlated with burnout potential (Bitcon, 1981). When there is no safe place in an organization to express negative feelings or no safe person with whom one can talk out situations that aroused negative feelings, then the capacity to deal effectively with suppression of feelings in order to adequately perform one's job becomes much more problematic.

Role Ambiguity

Role ambiguity can be defined as vagueness concerning job expectations or responsibilities and has been identified as a primary factor contributing to burnout (Cherniss, 1982; Maher, 1983; Potter, 1980; Richardson and West, 1982; Rosenthal et al., 1983). When individual goals and organizational objectives are unclear or when the parameters of the job and the scope of responsibility are undefined, chronic stress can result. Role ambiguity may also be the result of vague directives from administration or uncertainty as to how a particular job fits into the organization. All these facets of role ambiguity have been found to correlate highly with burnout (Potter, 1980).

Role ambiguity is increased in professions like librarianship, where rapid technological change occurs or where fiscal retrenchment is frequently encountered. The skills required for competent performance, the scope of responsibilities, and task priorities are especially influenced by fluctuations in financial support or changes in technology. As a result, individual roles are more likely to become uncertain. Studies have shown that the newest members of the staff, who are eager to do well and who are struggling to define what is expected of them, are most likely to be affected and to experience a significant level of role ambiguity (Daniels, 1985; Melendez and Guzman, 1983).

An additional cause of role ambiguity is particularly pertinent to librarianship. This is the continuous accretion of secondary responsibilities until it is difficult to determine what the primary role is. Persons who have difficulty saying no may find themselves in this situation, but this problem also arises when financial retrenchment has resulted in staff cuts or a hiring freeze. Both of these factors operate in libraries where, in addition, the increasing complexity of information science continues to add new responsibilities to professional roles.

Decreased Opportunities for Personal Accomplishment

Job satisfaction is a primary intrinsic motivator for many professionals. When opportunities for personal accomplishment are decreased, job satisfaction is likely to decrease as well, and many authors have found this decreased job satisfaction to be related to burnout (Bitcon, 1981; Melendez and Guzman, 1983; Perlman and Hartman, 1982). Corporate managers identified personal accomplishment as a primary motivation for their work (Pines and Aronson, 1988).

In many libraries, time for professional research, writing activities, or teaching activities is extremely limited or entirely absent. Sometimes work pressures are too great to allow the "luxury" of time for these professional endeavors, and occasionally cost factors prohibit them from being supported within the organization. In some libraries administrators place a lower value on these activities than on more traditional reference or technical services. Such limitations narrow the scope for a librarian to find a sense of personal accomplishment and may contribute to a decrease in job or career satisfaction.

An additional factor that can inhibit a sense of personal accomplishment and job satisfaction is lack of criteria for measuring accomplishments. Many tasks in libraries are only quantitatively measurable, with qualitative value much more difficult to ascertain. In addition, most library responsibilities are ongoing and dynamic, making it difficult to find a static point for appropriate measurement. Thus collection development efforts, public service tasks, and usefulness of technical services systems may be difficult to measure, and thus these endeavors provide less sense of personal accomplishment than completing an annual report, finalizing a budget, or completing a publication.

Inadequate Positive Feedback

One of the most frequently cited factors in burnout is a distinct lack of adequate positive feedback for one's efforts (Elliott and Smith, 1984; Melendez and Guzman, 1983; Perlman and Hartman, 1982; Pines and Aronson, 1988; Potter, 1980; Richardson and West, 1982). Sources for recognition of high-quality performance vary within the formal and informal structures of the organization. Librarians might get feedback from supervisors, colleagues, or patrons. The source of positive feedback has been shown to be less relevant than the quantity of feedback, however. If a supervisor never shows appreciation of a librarian's efforts, but colleagues and patrons do, the supervisor's lack of appreciation can be perceived as a fault in the supervisor rather than in the librarian and is less likely to promote burnout. If appreciation is more generally lacking and no one voices positive recognition, it is tempting to perceive a lack in oneself, with a concomitant decrease in self-esteem. This attitude is quite likely to promote burnout over the long term.

In libraries, positive feedback from patrons can be quite scarce, even when obvious satisfaction of information needs occurs. Indeed, many patrons take good library service for granted and are likely to provide feedback only when they are dissatisfied or unhappy with the service (Haack, Jones, and Roose, 1984). This is true of other helping professions as well: Professionals may be the recipients of complaints about the job they are doing, they may be blamed for not providing enough help, or they may even be the targets of hostile remarks or threatening actions. Sometimes, negative feedback is used as a deliberate strategy to speed up service. Lack of positive feedback is most likely in those professions in which the helper's accomplishments are regarded as part of the job (Maslach, 1982). For example, reference librarians are *expected* to provide answers; they rarely hear applause or congratulations for meeting this standard, although courtesy may prompt some acknowledgment of the assistance in the form of a "Thank you." When the standard is not met, however, the likelihood of expressed dissatisfaction can be very high. As noted by Ferriero and Powers (1982):

> Reference service has an inherent lack of positive feedback, either on how you are performing, or on how satisfied users are with your services. For anyone, but especially for a burned-out

librarian, it is almost impossible to replenish your vitality and
energy solely from user contact. (p. 275)

Lack of Control over Library Operations

Most professionals want to feel that their endeavors have a
significant (usually positive) impact on the organization in which
they work. Frequently cited work stressors include having too little
authority to make an impact, having to fight political pressures
that limit one's ability to have an impact, or not having full
information from upper administrative levels to enhance the possibility of making a positive impact (Bitcon, 1981; Elliot and
Smith, 1984; Maher, 1983; Pines and Aronson, 1988). Libraries, as
increasingly complex bureaucratic organizations, are vulnerable to
all of these conditions, which may help promote burnout.

Control is not distributed equally in organizations, which are
hierarchical to varying degrees and which tend to allocate much
control to a few and little control to many. Yet psychologists have
found that a feeling of some control is necessary for healthy
functioning, which means that staff members are more likely to
experience stress than managers, who have increased opportunities
for control. The exceptions are middle managers, who have been
found to be more susceptible to burnout than managers at other
levels, a fact fully consistent with data showing that most middle
managers have more responsibility than authority; in other words,
they have too little control (Potter, 1980). According to Ferriero
and Powers (1982), public service librarians also feel caught in a
middle position, feeling a lack of control over policies and procedures that directly affect users while simultaneously serving as the
most visible link between those users and the library decision
makers. The authors suggest that this literally puts public service
librarians in a position of having to defend, explain, or attempt to
circumvent policies into which they had little, if any, input and in
which they feel little confidence.

No-Win Situations

There are a wide variety of no-win situations, but the concept
of inadequacy is generally the operative factor in them. In most
no-win situations, the job to be done is clearly outlined and within
the individual's level of skill, but support resources are inadequate

to allow the job to actually be accomplished. The inadequate resources could be too few support staff available, too little time, too little money, or insufficient materials. Occasionally, a personal feeling of inadequacy may arise when a professional feels insufficiently trained for a particular task or role. When adequate resources are not available, the responsible professional experiences dissonance between what ought to be done and what can be done, and this dissonance is generally felt as increased stress and tension (Pines, 1982). In a survey investigating burnout among librarians, Haack, Jones, and Roose (1984) cite budget cuts and technological changes as primary work stressors in the library environment. Budgetary cuts directly produce a no-win situation by limiting resources. Technological change requires continuing education or new training to gain adequate competency.

Conflicting demands can create no-win situations, too. In this case, however, the expectations are very clear and the resources are adequate. The problem is that meeting one need necessarily results in failing to satisfy another. That means every "win" is accompanied by an inevitable "loss." Quality versus quantity issues often emerge in this light. High-quality performance frequently takes more time and decreases the quantity of a service, but focusing on speed to increase quantity can jeopardize quality (Potter, 1980). For example, a librarian may be asked to select materials on which to spend funds from an unexpected donation at the end of a budget year, with the caveat that if the money is not spent by the end of the year it will be lost. If too much time is taken to select expenditures wisely, too few purchases are made; when rapid purchase decisions are made, some needs can easily be overlooked. Other situations create conflicting demands as well. In small libraries with limited staff, every moment spent on providing patron-demand public service necessarily decreases the available time for collection development and technical organization of the library's materials. Without an appropriate collection and a good retrieval system, public services necessarily suffer. If a librarian neglects either task for the other, one service temporarily "wins" but in the long term everyone loses, staff and patrons alike.

One other no-win situation deserves recognition here, as it perpetuates a cycle of burnout within an organization that can contribute to the creation of an essentially unhealthy environment for everyone. Occasionally, persons who have been experiencing burnout will seek to alleviate it by seeking additional training and moving up administratively in their given profession. Although this may sound promising, research has shown that it is rarely, if ever, an effective means of alleviating or reversing the burnout process (Pines and Aronson, 1988). Instead, the burned-out worker becomes a burned-out supervisor who begins to contribute to the burnout process in the younger members of the staff. The end result: A new source of no-win situations can blossom. Frequently, the supervisor has a tendency to overpolice subordinates and provide a plethora of negative feedback, usually in the form of a continuous stream of criticism, which becomes a source of chronic stress and promotes more burnout (Bitcon, 1981).

Continuously Heavy Workload

Too many hours on the job, too many responsibilities to cover, too many individual tasks to handle, too much paperwork, and too many repetitive tasks have all been identified as workload stressors contributing to burnout (Daniels, 1985; Elliott and Smith, 1984; Maher, 1983; Matteson and Ivancevich, 1982; Perlman and Hartman, 1982; Pines, 1982; Rader, 1981; Zastrow, 1984). In libraries, an additional stressor is the frequent need to perform more than one task at a time (Haack, Jones, and Roose, 1984). Librarians may need to handle multiple reference requests at once or try to perform collection development tasks while serving a rotation at the reference desk. In technical services, availability of terminals or specific online services may require disruption of some tasks in order to perform others requiring technological support. In addition, these factors can contribute to an increased isolation from colleagues and a decreased social life as the work overload consumes more and more time. Two potential avenues of stress reduction (support from peers and friends) are thus restricted, making burnout more likely.

Work overload by itself is a stressor, but it is not the sole cause of burnout. Stress increases when people feel harried and behind schedule, worrying about deadlines (the line after which death occurs!) and having too many tasks to do in the time available. But studies have shown that attitude toward workload has an effect on the amount of stress experienced, and methods of dealing with stress and reducing burnout (detailed in Chapter 6) include changing one's perceptions of the impossible workload

(Potter, 1982). A more positive and more realistic view is actually a healthier view.

Stressors in the Physical Environment

All of the previously reviewed environmental stressors are psychosocial in nature, and the literature clearly suggests that the nature of work-related social interaction is a primary factor in whether or not burnout occurs. However, numerous studies describe other environmental stressors related entirely to physical properties of the environment that can play a significant role in increasing work-related tension. Although these are not generally considered primary factors in burnout, they are important to consider, as stress is a cumulative process. Physical stressors can therefore contribute to maintaining a continuously high level of stress and increasing the possibility of burnout. In addition, these are factors that may be amenable to change, thereby reducing or perhaps ameliorating some of the work-related stress that is felt by the individual.

Poor ventilation, poor lighting, excessive noise, lack of privacy, frequent interruptions, uncomfortable seating, and unavailability of lounge facilities are some of the many physical factors contributing to work-related stress (Melendez and Guzman, 1983; Richardson and West, 1982).

PERSONAL CAUSES OF BURNOUT

As noted earlier, the work environment is only half of the chronic stress formula that eventually results in burnout. The other half is within the individual person. One's dreams, hopes, thoughts, and actions can help or hinder the burnout process, making one more or less vulnerable to this uncomfortable and distressing phenomenon. Justice, Gold, and Klein (1981) found several common personality traits among individuals who experienced burnout. Specifically, overcommitment, excessive dedication, and lack of separation of oneself from one's work were found to be etiological for burnout.

High Idealism

Tragically, research shows that burnout is most likely among those who enter the helping professions with the highest ideals and the most enthusiasm. Students who are somewhat cynical by graduation are far less prone to burnout. Those who maintain a strong desire to give of themselves, to help others, and, in so doing, to make the world a better place for all people are most at risk (Pines and Aronson, 1988). And the more unrealistic one's expectations, the more likely one is to experience burnout (Zastrow, 1984). Generalized idealistic goals, such as "I want to make the world a better place," are also highly related to the burnout process (Maher, 1983; Maslach, 1982). Librarians may hold idealistic (and irrational) beliefs, such as "I will be able to help all the patrons who request services," "I will be highly appreciated by my supervisor, library, and patrons," "I will be able to substantially improve the provision of information services within my organization," or "I will advance rapidly and earn a high status commensurate with my education and work."

Perfectionism: The Fast Road to Librarian Burnout

People are unique, and their uniqueness has an impact on their potential for burnout. The tendency to strive for perfection can be translated into a wholesome work ethic of doing one's best on every task undertaken, no matter how small. But when a tendency toward perfectionism becomes a need for perfection, the result is perpetual frustration. Human beings are not perfect, and a need to be 100 percent perfect 100 percent of the time is inevitably problematic. When this drive to be perfect is applied to library work, the result is librarian burnout. The following first-person account is excerpted from an article by Jannean Elliott and Nathan Smith (1984). It articulately and poignantly describes the role of perfectionism in setting up unrealistic expectations as a primary factor in the burnout experience of a junior high school librarian.

> I had quite a few successes and rewards that year, mostly from the students, but I will concentrate on the reasons that I requested to return to the classroom as a teacher after just one year in the library.

First and foremost was my own perfectionism; I did it to myself. I felt I had to be the *best* all-round school librarian the world has ever seen. My library should be decorated and neat at all times. My files should be perfect and replete with every tiny piece of trivia you can imagine. I should teach library classes every week. I should also visit classes and give book talks. I should be open before school, during school, after school. I should have the best student worker program. I should have a flawless A-V department (machines and operations). I should know intimately every book in the library so I could recommend it; this means read, read, read. I should do my fair share of writing book reviews for the system. I should attend my professional meetings. I should chaperone school events and sponsor clubs in the name of student relations. I should be able to drop any work at any time in order to listen to teachers and students. I should juggle my miniature budget in such a way that the library is clearly growing and improving. . . . I should read my professional literature. I should hold special events such as book fairs. I should work with the PTA.

The list goes on ad nauseum. Looking back I realize how much of all that I really did accomplish most of the time and am amazed. But at the time all I could feel was guilt, guilt, guilt. I just felt I could never catch up with all that needed doing. By trying to be perfect in every area, I worked myself into the ground. . . .

Perfectionism! What a curse! And, I'm sure, a prime cause of burnout. (Elliott and Smith, 1984, p. 142)

Overcommitment

Overcommitment is another personal characteristic correlated with burnout. People who have a tendency toward perfectionism, have difficulty saying no, and have a strong need to compete with others may experience serious overcommitment of their personal resources, leading in time to burnout (Edelwich and Brodsky, 1980; Elliott and Smith, 1984; Freudenberger, 1977; Helliwell, 1981; Richardson and West, 1982). It is important to realize that striving for perfection guarantees only one result: perpetual frustration. At the least, there will be a series of continuing frustrations with rare instances of near-perfection briefly and sporadically achieved but which serve to reinforce people to continue the frustrating pursuit of perfection.

People who have a hard time saying no also find themselves becoming overcommitted easily. Having a tough time saying no suggests a person who may have too strong a need to please others and/or a tendency to base self-esteem on the external (and quite possibly inaccurate) opinions of other people. Finding other ways to measure self-worth, particularly ways that are internally defined rather than externally prescribed, may help in curbing a tendency to say yes too often.

Competition can also lead to overcommitment. Many studies suggest that a strong competitive drive masks an underlying fear of inadequacy. But overcommitting oneself, in the hope of achieving more and thus feeling more adequate, only leads to more failure and the exacerbation of underlying fears.

It is not uncommon for all three of the behaviors that characterize overcommitment to coexist in the same person. They all represent learned behaviors that encourage overextending one's resources in order to reach an unreachable standard, please other people, or beat out the other competition. Fortunately, all of the behaviors arising out of needs for being perfect, pleasing others, or proving oneself are learned and thus can be changed. Without change, they increase one's potential for burnout.

Single-mindedness

Pines and Aronson (1988) found that persons with a high potential for burnout are those

> for whom work is one of the most important things in life, if not the most important thing. It is what gives their lives a sense of meaning. They identify with their work and with the organization to such an extent that every success and every failure are personalized. Every sacrifice they (or in some cases their families) are required to make seems worth it. (p. 9)

As long as success is encountered more frequently than failure, these single-minded high achievers do well psychologically. However, when any other factors (and there are many possibilities) make success less frequent, they begin to experience the early stages of burnout. It doesn't matter whether or not these limiting factors are out of their control or not (for example, inadequate resources available to accomplish tasks and achieve success), work is so primary a part of their self-image that failure for any reason is intolerable. As success becomes more elusive, their single-mindedness increases, their sense of failure is heightened still more, and their personal burnout progresses.

Lack of Personal Support

The availability of personal support from colleagues, family, and friends has been found to be another factor that affects burnout. Persons who are more isolated and withdrawn are more prone to burnout, while those with wider social resources are less susceptible. Marriage helps: Studies have shown that married persons are somewhat less susceptible to burnout than single persons or persons in relationships representing alternative lifestyles such as cohabitation, triad relationships, and homosexuality (Maslach, 1982; Perlman and Hartman, 1982). Having children also helps: Childlessness was more highly correlated with burnout than parenthood (Maslach, 1982). Finally, the quality of extended family and social relationships matters: Maslach and Jackson (1979) report that poor relations with family and friends were frequently described by persons suffering from burnout.

Demographic Factors

Gender

Conflicting data on the correlation of gender and burnout have been found in several studies, and no definitive statement that either males or females are more prone to this phenomenon can be made at the present time. However, Maslach (1982) found that burned-out women were likely to experience more emotional exhaustion—felt more intensely—than burned-out men, and that burned-out men were more likely to experience feelings of depersonalization and distance from clients than burned-out women. Just being female or just being male neither enhances nor diminishes burnout potential. However, sex-role stereotyping continues to be a factor in occupational stress. When both men and women work in a profession that is stereotyped as essentially feminine or essentially masculine, they may encounter pressures to conform to the expectations generated by these strong occupational stereotypes. Thus, society may expect male librarians to be more effeminate than men in other types of business organizations, increasing the work-related stress of male librarians who do not fit this stereotype. At the same time, sexual stereotyping may predict that female librarians will be more successful in staff positions than in library management, increasing the work-related stress of the female librarian and arousing just as much anger and resentment as the unfairly stereotyped male feels. These societal expectations are sort of like white noise in the background—they may become familiar and be ignored, but they continue to provide a low-level stressor that contributes to the overall level of stress.

According to Elliott and Smith (1984), there also continue to be sociologically dictated job stress factors affecting working women, who are more likely than men to be underpaid, victimized by sexual harrassment, or left in a dead-end job with little hope of advancement. In addition, these authors say, working women still share the burden of having been raised from infancy to be sensitive to the needs of others, making them more likely to be rewarded at work with additional opportunities to meet the needs of others than to be moved into a position where others are expected to meet their needs. Other investigators have also identified sexism as a factor contributing to burnout and have suggested that this particular stressor may be as strong as role conflict, role ambiguity, or an unreasonably heavy workload (Zastrow, 1984).

Age

A clear relationship between age and burnout has been identified. Younger people are more likely to experience the burnout process than older people. Longevity on the job is also a factor that seems to correlate well with susceptibility to burnout. People with more job experience are less vulnerable to burnout, but chronological age seems to be a more important factor than seniority. This suggests that increased life experience provides individuals with significantly greater inner resources for coping with the stresses that promote burnout (Maslach, 1982; Perlman and Hartman, 1982). These findings from studies of general populations were also found to be true in a library population (Smith, Birch, and Marchant, 1986).

Education

Maslach (1982) found that people with a four-year college degree were most at risk for burnout, followed by individuals with postgraduate training. Those with less formal education appeared to suffer from burnout much less. Smith, Birch, and Marchant

(1986) found that librarians' potential for burnout increased with level of postgraduate education.

Employment

Full-time librarians are much more at risk for burnout than part-time librarians. In the same study, Smith, Birch, and Marchant (1986) found that only 4 to 14 percent of part-time librarians were suffering from burnout on the basis of scores signifying emotional exhaustion, while 23 to 25 percent of full-time librarians were experiencing burnout.

SUMMARY

In this chapter, the causes of burnout were reviewed. Numerous studies suggest that burnout potential is found both in the work environment and in individuals. Within the work environment, the most common stressors promoting burnout include decreased autonomy, role conflict, and role ambiguity. Decreased opportunities for personal accomplishment and inadequate positive feedback are also factors that promote burnout. Lack of control over system operations, no-win situations, continuously heavy workloads, and other physical stressors in the work environment correlated highly with the probability of burnout. Personal characteristics that increase susceptibility to burnout include high ideals, a tendency to overcommit oneself, and single-mindedness. Sex role stereotypes, experience of sexism, age (young), education (college degree), and hours of employment (full-time) were also identified as factors that could contribute to burnout.

Chapter 3
What Are the Signs and
Symptoms of Burnout?

In medicine, symptoms are what patients report they have noticed as unusual in the way they are feeling, thinking, or acting, and signs are what health care providers see in a professional examination of the patient. In the burnout process, signs may be noted by colleagues, supervisors, family, or friends long before the individual becomes aware of symptoms. It is thus important for everyone to be aware of what to watch for, even if a personal potential for burnout has not been identified.

Most people experience the signs and symptoms of burnout during their lifetime: These are feelings, behaviors, and somatic states that are a natural part of human existence. They do *not* indicate burnout unless the pattern is multiple. Many indicators need to be present concurrently. They should be continuously or repetitively experienced with few breaks in the pattern, and they should be associated with a significant decrease in job satisfaction. It is particularly important to note that the diagnostic criteria for burnout require that all three types of exhaustion—emotional, mental, and physical—must be experienced in response to continuously high levels of work-related stress before an individual is thought to be in the process of burning out.

Three major areas of burnout symptomatology have been identified: psychological, physical, and behavioral. Psychological symptoms include feelings, attitudes, and stress-induced neuropsychological dysfunctions such as decreased attention or concentration skills. Physical symptoms can range from relatively mild disorders to major cardiovascular difficulties. Behavioral symptoms include changes in patterns of interpersonal relations, work performance problems, or increased use of drugs or alcohol. They can range from the relatively minor habit of clock-watching to the significant and serious beginnings of suicidal ideation. Table 1 (page 30) lists the most frequently reported signs and symptoms of burnout.

PSYCHOLOGICAL SIGNS AND SYMPTOMS

When the burnout process begins, individuals experience significant changes in the way they feel about themselves, about others, and about events. Internally, they may notice increased tension or anxiety without being able to pinpoint other feelings that are also being aroused. Externally, other people frequently notice a change in attitude toward work or toward those with whom the burnout victims come in contact at work. Eventually, emotional disruption of cognitive functioning begins to be evident and the burning-out individuals become somewhat distractible. They also experience more difficulty in thinking problems through to appropriate solutions. Other people may notice that the burnout victims just don't appear as intellectually sharp as they used to be.

Feelings

A wide variety of feelings have been correlated with the burnout process. It is important to note that many burnout victims are so overwhelmed by the experience that they find it hard to differentiate specific feelings, making their early recognition of the feelings difficult and hampering their subsequent exploration of the underlying beliefs and events that generated the feelings.

Anger

Nearly every empirical study on burnout shows a high correlation with anger on the part of victims, who feel that they are unfairly treated by life. They essentially think life would be better for them if there was any justice in the world (Freudenberger and Richelson, 1980; Glicken, 1983; Justice, Gold, and Klein, 1981; Maher, 1983; Maslach, 1982; Potter, 1987; Stevens and Pfost, 1983). Anger is a logical response when idealistic persons find that hard work, loyalty, enthusiasm, and competence seem to be rewarded only by a constant stream of problems that deplete their emotional resources without appearing to make much difference in

TABLE 1: Signs and Symptoms of Burnout

PSYCHOLOGICAL	PHYSICAL	BEHAVIORAL
Feelings	*Mild Disorders*	*Interpersonal Relations*
anger	backaches	
anxiety	colds	blaming others
apathy	fatigue	conflicts with others
boredom	flu	criticizing others
depression	gastrointestinal	defensiveness
despair	problems	distancing from others
discouragement	hypersomnia	fault finding
disillusionment	insomnia	marital conflicts
dissatisfaction	malaise	withdrawal
fear	migraine headaches	
frustration	muscle tension	*Work Performance*
guilt	muscle weakness	
helpnessness	nausea	absenteeism
hopelessness	shortness of breath	clock-watching
irritability	tension headaches	decreased efficiency
pessimism	weight gain	increased mistakes
resentment	weight loss	living for breaks
suspicion		lowered standards
		obsessiveness
Attitudes	*Major Disorders*	overcommitment
	cerebral infarction	reliance on rules
cynicism	hypertension	tardiness
depersonalization	myocardial infarction	undercommitment
indifference		workaholism
moodiness		
resignation		*Substance Use*
self-doubt		
		alcoholism
		caffeine use
Neuropsychological dysfunction		drug abuse
		tobacco use
reduced attention		
reduced concentration		*Significant Behaviors*
reduced problem solving		
		accidents
		suicide
		unnecessary risks

terms of making the world a better place. A burned-out school librarian reported feeling anger approaching fury when she discovered that her fellow faculty members envied her for having an "easy job" when she was putting in close to seventy hours per week to keep up with the needs of her one-person operation.

Anger may turn to bitterness when individuals feel misunderstood or intentionally maligned by the system in which they work (Bitcon, 1981).

Anxiety

Anxiety ranges from a mildly unpleasant state to extreme discomfort and may also be known as concern, tension, worry, apprehension, nervousness, or panic. High levels of anxiety are difficult for individuals to tolerate for long periods, and most people use psychological defense mechanisms such as denial or repression to deal with anxiety. Denial allows one to refuse to feel overwhelmed by denying the severity of a situation, while repression allows one to safely ignore the feelings of tension until after the crisis has been met and dealt with successfully.

According to Muldary (1983), burnout victims characteristically use five specific defense mechanisms to deal with anxiety. First, intellectualization is used to seek emotional detachment by dealing with stressful events in abstract and intellectual terms. This is more difficult to do in later stages of burnout when cognitive disruptions are common and self-esteem is too low to be consonant with the facade of intellectualism. Reaction formation and rationalization, the second and third defenses Muldary found in burnout victims, are attempts to deal both with the anxiety-producing situation and the stirrings of lowered self-esteem. In reaction formation, one attempts to conceal feelings by expressing their opposite (for example, a librarian who finds patrons irritating may express warm pleasure in working with people), while in rationalization, one attributes socially acceptable motives to actions in order to identify them with responsible and proper behavior (for example, the librarian who explains that she did everything possible to help the patron, but the patron was unwilling or unable to follow her directions accurately). Finally, Muldary found that burnout victims frequently used projection and displacement more than the general population. Projection is the attribution of one's own undesirable feelings to others, as when a librarian who is feeling threatened by the competency of a colleague accuses the colleague of being jealous or afraid of being outdone. Displacement is the redirection of feelings toward a person or object who is not not the source of the feelings. For example, a librarian who is angry about events at work may take out that anger on people at home. (This practice is sometimes called "kicking the dog.")

Again, high levels of anxiety have very commonly been reported as symptomatic of burnout (Justice, Gold, and Klein, 1981; Pines and Aronson, 1988; Potter, 1987; Simendinger and Moore, 1985; Zastrow, 1984).

Apathy

Work dissatisfaction can lead to an "I don't give a damn" attitude in persons who were once very committed and idealistic (Bitcon, 1981; Pines and Aronson, 1988). Armstrong (1978) reports that when apathy sets in, professionals stop returning phone calls from colleagues and clients and feel immobilized and helpless. In the library, apathy may be demonstrated when a library staff member appears far less motivated than in the past, showing little interest in the overall view of library service and plodding methodically along, doing each assigned task without interacting with others or appearing to care about quality performance. Lack of interest in accuracy and comprehensiveness may also be evident.

Boredom

Boredom begins to be experienced when cynicism increases in individuals experiencing burnout (Melendez and Guzman, 1983; Stevens and Pfost, 1983). They are natural companions, according to Freudenberger and Richelson (1980), because once a person begins to view the work world from the periphery rather than from the center, it's hard to stay interested in what's going on. Whether in the library or another work environment, boredom is demonstrated in similar ways—nonverbal behaviors such as yawning and stretching and having difficulty staying awake in meetings increase dramatically, and the person becomes stimulated only when nonwork topics are introduced.

Depression

Depression is very frequently reported by victims of burnout as a major factor in their emotional exhaustion (Glicken, 1983; Justice, Gold, and Klein, 1981; Potter, 1987; Zastrow, 1984). In the early stages of burnout, people are likely to experience worksite depression but relate quite happily when away from the work environment, making the depression experienced in early stages of burnout quite different from clinical depression, which is pervasive and experienced in all aspects of life. In the later and extreme stages of burnout, an individual may begin to experience significant amounts of self-blame for failing to deal with problems that appear entirely out of control and overwhelming, and clinical depression may evolve (Freudenberger and Richelson, 1980; Pines and Aronson, 1988). The depression of early burnout is generally specific to the work environment, and a librarian may feel totally enervated while on the job, but later play tennis or attend a concert quite comfortably. In clinical depression, which may be reached if burnout is severe and there is a sufficient belief that one is responsible for one's own burnout, the state of enervation exists in all areas of a person's life. The clinically depressed librarian who sits staring into space at work will sit staring into space at home as well.

Discouragement, Disillusionment, and Despair

Pines and Aronson (1988) report that significant amounts of discouragement were reported by various types of professionals undergoing burnout, particularly after they experienced a sense of disillusionment when the high ideals they held as students were too discrepant from the realities of the work world. These same authors note that despair is an extreme form of discouragement in which the hope that one can have an impact on the problematic situation is essentially extinguished.

Dissatisfaction

Plate and Stone (1976) investigated librarian job satisfaction and found that a sense of achievement and recognition are primary determining factors. When these needs are not met, librarians experience a high degree of job dissatisfaction, which is an integral part of the definition of burnout. People in later stages of the burnout process noted that the feeling of job dissatisfaction generalized and expanded until it appeared to permeate other facets of their life as well. All relationships and activities became less satisfying (Glicken, 1983; Justice, Gold, and Klein, 1981). Librarians who become disenchanted with library work and seek new challenges or careers may find themselves becoming rapidly disappointed in these new endeavors as well unless they have made appropriate efforts to stop and reverse their burnout.

Fear

Fear is the anxiety generated by a perceived danger and is a realistic response to what is perceived as a true threat. Muldary (1983) reported fear as a symptom of burnout, but other authors have not reported it.

Frustration

Confronting apparent barriers to the satisfaction of an individual's wants and needs is common throughout life. In small doses, frustration can be positively experienced as an effective motivator for problem solving. But high levels of frustration that are experienced in the form of continuous and unresolvable barriers that keep one from the successful completion of job responsibilities is a sign of burnout. Bitcon (1981) notes that continuous frustration requires constant readaptation to situations and events, and that this effort is a great source of exhaustion. Generally, what are initially recognized as intense feelings of job dissatisfaction in time lead many burnout victims to blame themselves for their inability to overcome frustrations, and a sense of futility and reduced self-esteem also result (Potter, 1980). Librarians who experience high levels of frustration may begin to view themselves as inadequate, especially if the same conditions don't appear to be affecting others as badly. Feelings of inadequacy combined with a sense of futility engendered by rarely (or never) overcoming frustrating barriers can lead to a sense of failure both as a librarian and as a person.

Guilt

Maslach (1982) reports that most people regard burnout as a reflection of some basic personality malfunction and that this belief propels them into some form of self-condemnation. Instead of recognizing that their assigned workload is truly impossible, they blame themselves for not being able to figure out a way to handle it. Psychologists have long been aware of a tendency called the "fundamental attribution error" in which people overestimate personal factors and underestimate situational factors. Simply stated, it is more ego boosting to think of oneself as in control of the environment than to think that the environment may be in control. Unfortunately, when environmental factors create an impossible situation, people are caught in a trap that encourages them to take personal responsibility for the loss of control generated by the environment.

Helplessness and Hopelessness

The failure to escape from continuous stress despite one's efforts to alleviate it or control the situation eventually teaches the individual that *nothing* effective can be done. At this point, laboratory studies have shown, a mind-set of "learned helplessness" begins. Individuals essentially learn that their efforts are bound to be ineffective, and they stop trying to improve the situation and simply strive for passive survival. This is learned helplessness. When hopelessness, the final stage of learned helplessness, is reached, even passive survival seems too great an effort. Burnout victims have reported both symptoms (Pines and Aronson, 1988). Librarians who display learned helplessness may simply accept each new stress without bothering even to complain. They are likely to be indecisive and have difficulty establishing priorities or managing time well.

Irritability

According to Maslach (1982), irritable people are impulsive, impatient, and intolerant and are much more prone to burnout than others. She reports that emotional exhaustion is most likely very high, even if mental and physical exhaustion is still relatively mild, when a persistent irritability is demonstrated as a primary sign of burnout. Freudenberger and Richelson (1980) note that impatience is a usual characteristic of the competent and enthusiastic people who are prime candidates for burnout. With a vast supply of energy and a high level of skill, they are used to doing things well and quickly. When the first signs of burnout appear, their impatience grows and soon erupts into irritability with themselves and with everyone around them.

Pessimism

Another symptom reported by burnout victims is a growing sense of pessimism because coping with constant problems can run down the batteries of even the most enthusiastic people, leading them to expect negative outcomes more frequently (Potter, 1980).

Resentment

When burnout is recognized, an alternative to self-blame for the burnout phenomenon is to blame the other person in the relationship (Maslach, 1982). Librarians may blame problem patrons, teachers may blame unmanageable students, and social workers may blame their clients or the legal system. "I'm burning out because of *them*." The idea is that other people are always doing something (they're always complaining, causing trouble, breaking the rules, etc.) and if only *they* would stop, *I* would be just fine.

Suspicion

Individuals who are burning out are generally not the first to recognize that they have a problem; they may also be unaware that the quality of their work is decreasing. When less positive reinforcement is forthcoming from supervisors and colleagues, burnout victims begin to wonder why. They may become suspicious of their managers or peers, wondering if someone is intentionally trying to cause them a career injury (Bitcon, 1981; Justice, Gold, and Klein, 1981; Maher, 1983; Melendez and Guzman, 1983). Freudenberger and Richelson (1980) note that it is a small step from growing suspicion to paranoia and suggest that burnout victims may become highly mistrustful.

Attitudes

The development of negative attitudes, particularly toward other people, is one of the most dramatic and early symptoms of burnout. An attitude can be defined as a preexisting mind-set to act in a certain way toward a particular object, event, or person—a sort of mental readiness to produce a specific response. Negative attitudes of various types are common to burnout, and the individuals who experience the phenomenon may find changes in their mind-set difficult to tolerate and threatening to their self-esteem. However, other people view the burnout victims' negative attitudes as generally less important than the behaviors that are induced by the attitudes, as these behaviors are most likely to have a primary effect on others (Muldary, 1983). Librarians who develop a negative attitude toward patrons may be brusque, condescending, or hostile when approached. Patrons notice and react to these behaviors and logically conclude that a negative attitude lies behind them. Librarians in earlier stages of burnout may effectively hide their changed attitude if they remain socially skilled for a period of time, carefully controlling their behavior. Maintaining controlled behavior is difficult, however. It requires constant vigilance and effort, both of which burning out individuals have in ever shorter supply. Eventually, the new negative attitude is out on public display. The lead-in to an article on librarian burnout by Ferriero and Powers (1982) is a good illustration of how a negative attitude grows and finally gets expressed:

> If I don't get away from this desk soon . . . another dumb question . . . I never have time to do my own work, it's so busy here at the desk . . . This is so boring . . . only the complainers comment on my work . . . I should have helped that person more, but I'm exhausted . . . I know I shouldn't snap at the users but I can only do so much . . . If that phone doesn't stop ringing I'm going to scream . . . Rules are rules and we're not going to bend them for anyone . . . Lady, I don't really care where today's papers are. (p. 274)

Cynicism

Most of the major research studies on burnout have reported that persons suffering from the syndrome experience an increasing cynicism, or worldly weariness, about their work. The high ideals they once held become so tarnished that these values are unrecognizable and may be totally discarded. By this point, the burnout victims assume that a change in their stressors is not simply unlikely, it is impossible. Hope dies, and a belief that no one can improve "the system" grows ever stronger (Freudenberger and Richelson, 1980; Maslach, 1982; Pines and Aronson, 1988; Potter, 1987). Naturally, the demise of hope breeds an increasing depression and apathy. In late stages of burnout, the victims are living very uncomfortable lives in every sense of the word: They are not only sorely distressed, but no sources of relief and comfort seem to exist.

Depersonalization

Maslach (1982) calls depersonalization "a virtual hallmark of the burnout syndrome" (p. 17). In depersonalization, a shift in attitude from positive and caring to negative and uncaring occurs on the caregiver's part. Service providers may develop low opinions of clients' capabilities, may describe them in derogatory terms, and may undervalue them as individuals. Illustrative statements might be "I can't believe the weirdos we get around here" or "You'd think they were born in a cave and raised by wolves."

Indifference

When people feel let down by others or by their work environment, they experience a need to protect themselves from the pain of feeling abandoned or betrayed. One effective defense is a facade of indifference, a sort of "sour grapes" stance. If you tell yourself "I don't care; it wasn't important anyway," you can lessen the pain caused by caring. This detachment can be protective when you're feeling emotionally exhausted, but it is ineffective and counterproductive in resolving the problem. At a time when peer support would be helpful and desirable, it is less likely to be sought if you convince yourself of how little the disappointment really matters. Isolation, rather than camaraderie, is the net effect of feigning indifference, and burnout progresses faster in people who feel isolated and alone than it does in people who feel supported by others (Freudenberger and Richelson, 1980; Potter, 1987).

Lowered Self-Esteem

Burnout arouses so many feelings of inadequacy, incompetence, ineffectiveness, and inferiority that it is not at all surprising that burnout victims begin to doubt their value as individuals. Believing themselves unable to make a difference, they put in the hours necessary to take a paycheck home and feel increasingly empty and useless (Muldary, 1983). Behaviorally, the early signs of lowered self-esteem may be seen in librarians who no longer volunteer to be involved in projects, who begin to make self-denigrating remarks, or who greet most organizational goals with the belief that "it won't make any difference to me." Other signs of reduced self-esteem include less attention to hygiene or personal appearance. Women may no longer wear makeup or jewelry, and men may appear more often without a jacket or tie. The once well-groomed, business-like appearance of the librarian go-getter may turn into a very casual look more suitable to Saturday grocery shopping than library service.

Problems seem much more insurmountable to people who suffer from reduced self-esteem. Any small snafu or minor setback can and usually is perceived as a major crisis. People become less willing to try to overcome these obstacles and are more willing to give up in despair (Maslach, 1982). Of course, this becomes a vicious circle, because the less you try to overcome an obstacle, the less likely you are to succeed in doing so, and the greater the obstacle looms in your mind. Without success to balance the scale, the self-denigration process can continue unchallenged. From a stance of "Why bother? I couldn't handle it right anyway" the transition to "I *knew* I couldn't do it" is very easy.

Moodiness

Although Potter (1980) believes that moodiness is a feeling of emotional tautness that signals impending burnout, other authors do not attach the same significance to moodiness, and few define it specifically as a symptom of burnout. Moodiness does not appear to be a true attitude in terms of a mind-set as defined above, either. However, it appears that moodiness can be identified as a sign of burnout that supervisors, family, colleagues, and friends of the victim may observe. Moodiness is demonstrated as a seemingly random pattern of expression of other symptoms of burnout, such as detachment, anger, withdrawal, irritability, or apathy. These fluctuations of a burnout victim's emotional state appear as alternating and, more important, unpredictable changes of mood that are strong enough to disrupt work performance and interpersonal relationships.

Resignation

Muldary (1983) suggests that burnout victims experience a passive resignation to the system, making few efforts to leave it or reform it. No other study reports this particular symptom, but it is so close to the concept of learned helplessness that it appears to be simply a semantic difference.

Self-doubt

As self-esteem is reduced, persons experiencing burnout report a strong tendency to question the value of their work, doubting it is good enough but feeling unable to improve it (Stevens and Pfost, 1983). Once again, a vicious circle begins. When you think your work is faulty, but you can't see how to improve it, your opinion of your work and of yourself continues to decline. Of course, the worse you feel about yourself, the less able you are to take effective action.

Neuropsychological Dysfunction

Clinical psychologists and neuropsychologists have long known that emotions can effectively disrupt cognitive functions in clearly measurable ways. Test results in innumerable psychological evaluations have repeatedly shown this quantitatively. Qualitatively, it is easy to understand this phenomenon, as it happens to all of us occasionally. For example, anxiety has a specific effect on memory, as anyone who really needs to remember something elusive can confirm. The harder you try, the farther away the memory seems to slip; then, just as you relax and stop worrying about remembering, zing! the memory pops up clear as a bell. Burnout investigations show that mental exhaustion is frequently demonstrated in decreases in attention and concentration, memory skills, judgment, and problem solving skills (Cherniss, 1980; Muldary, 1983).

Reduced Attention and Concentration

Simple attentional skills are among the first cognitive functions to be affected by burnout. People experiencing the burnout phenomenon find that their attention wanders easily, that they are easily distracted from work by sights and sounds, and that it is more difficult than it used to be to get themselves back on track quickly or effectively. The more complex task of maintaining attention and mentally manipulating concepts and ideas through concentrated effort is also disrupted in burnout (Paine, 1984; Potter, 1987). Librarians may report jumping from task to task without ever finishing any, or finding themselves following a new train of thought when it strikes them instead of staying with the task at hand. They may have difficulty attending to complicated reference questions or meeting agendas and may lose the thread of conversations easily.

Reduced Problem Solving

The task of problem solving is a highly complex one that requires logic and reasoning superimposed on learning habits. To solve problems, people have to mentally manipulate ideas, perceptions, and concepts within a framework of past experiences, logic, habits and rules. Logical progressions and intuitive leaps in thinking frequently occur, and creative thought is required to consider new alternatives for situations that may never have been met before. Most professionals are skilled and practiced at problem solving and can automatically engage in the process with little effort, sometimes without even realizing a conscious need to do so or recognizing that they have started. However, as the burnout process progresses, individuals are less able to engage in problem solving with this automatic and often minimal effort. Problems are thus harder for burnout victims to solve. Of course, this increases anxiety as the burnout victims realize that solutions are becoming more elusive. Under ordinary circumstances, a mild level of anxiety tends to facilitate rather than inhibit problem solving, but when anxiety is significantly heightened, this tendency reverses. It is not uncommon for burnout victims to begin worrying so much over difficulties with problem solving that they quite literally make themselves incapable of dealing with the problem through worrying over the process (Muldary, 1983). Paine (1984) reports that people suffering from burnout experience a cognitive rigidity or mental inflexibility that inhibits their creative problem-solving skills.

Impaired Judgment

When attention and concentration skills and the capacity for problem solving are reduced, the result is likely to be impaired judgment. Even when people have the capacity to make sound judgments, they are unlikely to do so unless they have good data. In burnout, inattention and mental inflexibility have an inhibitory effect on the data collected in order to make judgments, and the chance of making sound decisions is thus significantly reduced (Paine, 1984). Ferriero and Powers (1982) reported that burned-out reference librarians had difficulty distinguishing between productive and nonproductive efforts, and made poor judgments when faced with choices on what they should do.

Disorientation

In severe burnout, episodic mental confusion may occur. Victims may lose track of where they are and where they are supposed to be, or they may lose track of time (Freudenberger and Richelson, 1980). Everyone loses track of time sometimes—especially under emotional conditions. When at a party having fun, one may check the time and be astonished to discover it is much later than expected. Time really does fly when one is having fun. The reverse is also common; time may drag painfully when one is worried about something or someone. The time a master's thesis committee takes to deliberate on one's success or failure can feel like a lifetime. For most people, these experiences are short-lived and their usual time sense functions the majority of the time. In burnout, it can feel as if these elastic qualities of time are continuous, with little return of one's usual time sense.

PHYSICAL SIGNS AND SYMPTOMS

Some people respond to stress by developing physical illnesses that allow them to focus on somatic concerns, diverting their attention from the events that have increased their stress levels. It must be noted that stress-induced illnesses are no less physical than other illnesses. Stress-induced disorders have recognizable physical effects, regardless of their origin. According to Selye (1956), everyone experiences stress as a demand for a physiological response from the body. In some people, stress reduces the efficiency of their immune systems, making them more susceptible to infection. Sometimes stress serves to exacerbate preexisting conditions such as allergies, and sometimes stress levels are high enough for a sufficient period of time to produce long-lasting effects of prolonged physiological imbalance, such as ulcers or hypertension.

Psychogenic illnesses (sometimes referred to as psychosomatic disorders) are true illnesses with real pain and true physiological changes. When illnesses are defined as psychogenic, some people react by experiencing extreme cognitive dissonance and seeking specific physical etiologies for their symptoms in an attempt to deny psychological involvement. Others are able to treat the difficulties psychologically. Regardless of the individual's response, the recognition of psychogenic illness as a real and distressing experience is important in the identification and treatment of burnout. Burnout victims can easily be tempted to view work-related psychogenic illnesses as socially acceptable reasons to remove themselves from the work environment. This avoidance may become a secondary gain of great value to victims of burnout, and seeking treatment for the burnout syndrome itself may become less appealing. If simple avoidance of the work environment was sufficient to combat burnout, then treatment by leave of absence is reasonable. But avoidance alleviates the problem only temporarily. As soon as the same (or new) stressors reappear, the burnout process resumes. Occupational medicine studies have shown that 10 percent of the workforce experiences up to 80 percent of the illnesses (Pfifferling and Eckel, 1982), suggesting a particular need to seek effective stress management techniques for that 10 percent of the workforce.

Mild Disorders

A wide variety of mild physical disorders have been correlated with burnout. These include development of new problems never before experienced, reappearance of problems previously experienced, and exacerbation of ongoing problems. Calling these disorders mild may suggest that they are little more than annoyances, but this is not true. They are mild only because they are not generally life-threatening. The irritation and pain experienced by many sufferers is far from mild.

Backaches, Shoulder Aches, and Neck Pain

Low back pain, neck pain, and shoulder pain are frequently reported by people experiencing significant stress levels, and the burnout studies also show a high frequency of these complaints among sufferers of burnout (Justice, Gold, and Klein, 1981; Pines and Aronson, 1988; Potter, 1987).

Colds

Burnout victims have more colds than the general population and may also experience lingering cold symptoms long after others with the same type of infection have fully recovered (Justice, Gold, and Klein, 1981; Pines and Aronson, 1988; Potter, 1980, 1987; Stevens and Pfost, 1983; Tanner, 1983; Zastrow, 1984).

Exacerbation of Allergies

Allergy attacks are more common and allergy symptoms are more evident in burnout victims than in people with known allergies who are not experiencing burnout (Paine, 1984; Potter, 1980).

Fatigue

Physical exhaustion is a major component of the burnout syndrome, and sufferers begin by reporting unusual fatigue at the end of the workday. "I don't know what's wrong with me. I just feel wiped out." Excessive fatigue gradually progresses to a more generalized feeling of never getting enough rest. This symptom is reported in all the major burnout research studies, without exception.

Flu and Gastrointestinal Problems

Burnout victims also appear to be more susceptible to recurrent or lingering bouts of intestinal flu (Pines and Aronson, 1988; Potter, 1980; Stevens and Pfost, 1983; Visotsky and Cramer, 1982). A variety of non-influenza gastrointestinal complaints also have been reported by burnout victims, including abdominal cramps, bowel dysfunctions, and ulcers (Justice, Gold, and Klein, 1981; Maslach, 1982; Paine, 1984; Stevens and Pfost, 1983)

Insomnia

Many burnout victims report difficulties getting to sleep or staying asleep (Glicken, 1983; Justice, Gold, and Klein, 1981; Maher, 1983; Potter, 1980, 1987; Simendinger and Moore, 1985; Stevens and Pfost, 1983; Zastrow, 1984). A night or two of insomnia makes many people tired enough to ensure some following nights of repose. Burnout victims, however, consistently report coinciding daytime weariness and continued nighttime insomnia (Pines and Aronson, 1988). More rarely, burnout victims have reported hypersomnia, an inability to awaken easily and a need for excessive amounts of sleep (Stevens and Pfost, 1983).

Migraine and Tension Headaches

Headaches are another symptom frequently reported by burnout victims. These seem to occur relatively early in the process and may initially be specifically associated with work hours or times spent thinking about problems at work. In later stages of burnout, the headache has either become a nearly continuous occurrence, generalized from work activities to all facets of life, or it has been superseded by other symptoms (Glicken, 1983; Justice, Gold, and Klein, 1981; Maher, 1983; Maslach, 1982; Pines and Aronson, 1988; Potter, 1987; Stevens and Pfost, 1983; Tanner, 1983; Zastrow, 1984).

Muscle Tension and Weakness

Pain from muscle tension and subsequent feelings of weakness in certain muscle groups have also been reported as symptoms of burnout (Muldary, 1983; Paine, 1984). Muscle tension may show up as trembling, nervous tics, stuttering, clenched jaws or fists, increased urinary urgency, tight feelings in the chest or stomach, or a weak feeling in the knees.

Shortness of Breath

Although a variety of respiratory problems have been reported in stress studies, the burnout investigations have not reported significant difficulties of this type, with one exception. Justice, Gold, and Klein (1981) reported that burnout victims experienced shortness of breath, particularly when anxiety levels were high.

Weight Gain or Loss

People who are attempting to deal with increased stresses and depleted reserves frequently seek the comfort of early types of nurturing experiences, such as food intake (Pines and Aronson, 1988). Everyone must eat, and a great many people find particular pleasure in dining activities, but an overabundance of eating be- haviors can lead to an unhealthy gain in body weight. Some of the literature on obesity and stress suggests that the human body deals differently with caloric intake in periods of stress, making weight gain somewhat more likely at these times than at others (Pennebaker, 1982). In addition, Maslach (1982) reports that in- creased consumption of fast foods in an effort to minimize meal preparation and dining time is common in early stages of burnout, when people are still trying desperately to cope with increased work demands. The consumption of fast food and easily obtained snack items in place of balanced meals can also lead to weight gain.

For some burnout victims, increased consumption of food occurs. As mentioned previously, early nurturing is frequently associated with food intake, and some individuals find eating to be a comforting behavior when they are dealing with stress. As one victim reported, "Eating was the only fun thing I was still able to do, so I just ate and ate" (Maslach, 1982, p. 102). Of course, unnecessary consumption of calories leads to weight gains and may lead to more serious consequences as well. Occasionally, the reverse occurs and burnout victims eat too little ("I just couldn't get anything past the lump in my throat from all the stress I had every day"). Again, serious consequences can result from consump- tion of too few calories and nutrients (Pines and Aronson, 1988).

Some people lose weight under stress. This may result from an increased metabolic rate, which causes calories to be burned more rapidly; it may also be the result of poor nutrition caused by an extended period in which food selection is poor in required nutrients. Similarly, people may lose weight because they skip meals in order to use the time for work. Finally, weight loss may occur because burnout victims feel too anxious or too sick to eat. As Selye (1956) pointed out, the human reaction to stress includes slowing of the digestive processes so that hunger will not interfere with the fight or flight response.

Major Disorders

Very serious illnesses can also result from prolonged high levels of stress. The relationship of increased stress and cardiovascular disease has been recognized for a long time. Pines and Aronson (1988) found that when general unemployment rises by 1 percent, there is a 1.9 percent increase in deaths from cardiovascular diseases and cirrhosis of the liver (attributed to excess alcohol consumption) over the next six years. Hypertension and heart attacks have been reported in the burnout literature as associated with severe cases of burnout (Justice, Gold, and Klein, 1981; Paine, 1984; Zastrow, 1984). McQuade and Aikman (1974) suggest that diabetes, cancer, and emphysema also can be significantly exacerbated by burnout.

BEHAVIORAL SIGNS AND SYMPTOMS

Once again, in the area of behavioral changes, a wide variety of signs and symptoms have been reported in burnout victims. Like the psychological and physical signs and symptoms, all of these behaviors occur in the general population who are not experiencing unusual job stresses. When they are preceded by, or run concurrently with, prolonged and excessive work-related stressors, they can be viewed as indicators that the burnout phenomenon is underway. Increased difficulties in interpersonal relationships, sometimes leading to the breakdown of even long-term relationships, are common signs of burnout. Deterioration of work performance is also especially frequent, as one might logically guess. Many authors suggest that substance abuse occurs as the result of burnout, although the directional nature of this relationship is questionable. Finally, behaviors with very serious consequences, such as suicide, have been reported among burnout victims.

Interpersonal Relationships

Burnout has a detrimental effect on interpersonal relationships. Negative feelings disrupt once good relations, and social skills deteriorate.

Blaming Others

When previously competent individuals begin to have difficulties, there is a strong temptation to assign blame to others rather than to themselves; otherwise they might have to admit unpleasant truths that are easier (and more comforting) to deny. Bitcon (1981) suggests that burnout sufferers do a fair amount of scapegoating, seeking to find other people who can be considered responsible for the problems they are experiencing.

Conflicts with Others

Conflict is an inevitable element of the human condition, but a significant increase in the number of conflicts or the frequency with which small conflicts escalate into larger ones, and a reduced ability to resolve conflicts, are regularly reported as symptoms of burnout (Muldary, 1983; Potter, 1980; Visotsky and Cramer, 1982).

Distancing from Others

The most outstanding and frequently cited symptom of burnout in members of the helping professions is an increased detachment from the clients they serve (Maslach, 1982; Muldary, 1983). Reduced concern for patron needs ("That ought to be enough for her—I don't feel like looking any further") and dehumanizing humor ("Oh-oh, here comes 'mad dog' Miller. Get ready for his bark!") may be demonstrated. Some people act out the distancing process through physical distancing, such as putting a desk or increased empty space between themselves and patrons or actually avoiding any contact, such as ducking out of sight into the rest room to avoid exchanging commonplaces with a colleague.

Marital and Family Conflicts

Although the burnout victim's stresses are work-related, many sufferers take their difficulties home with them. Over time, family and marital conflicts emerge. This not only increases the overall stress levels of the burnout victim, but it also produces new, indirect victims of burnout in the affected partners (Glicken, 1983; Justice, Gold, and Klein, 1981; Stevens and Pfost, 1983).

Withdrawal

Increasingly unsatisfactory interpersonal relationships, difficulties resolving conflicts, and a decrease in emotional support may result in an almost complete emotional withdrawal on the part of the burnout victim (Potter, 1980). Sometimes less emotional support is offered to burnout victims by other people who find the burnout victims difficult to deal with; at other times emotional support may be sought less by burnout victims who feel unworthy of it or who believe that the result will not be worth the effort. Emotional withdrawal is like insulation: It buffers emotional demands in order to provide a temporary sense of comfort in isolation. For the short term, this may be an effective way to deal with a situation. As a long-term response to ongoing stresses, however, it is simply ineffective because no changes in the situation result from it. Withdrawn individuals do not socialize with peers for breaks or at lunchtime, leave immediately when the workday is done, engage in little or no casual conversation with peers, may not offer the usual civil greeting such as "Good morning" unless spoken to first, and seat themselves in isolated areas when forced to participate in group meetings.

Work Performance

As emotional and mental exhaustion increases, burnout victims become less and less competent at work. They are also less motivated and make poor employees. Work performance may deteriorate dramatically as people who were once idealistic and perfectionistic hard workers stop caring about getting the job done at all.

Decreased Efficiency and Increased Mistakes

In the early stages of burnout, people continue to perform work functions fairly capably, although their speed or comprehensiveness may diminish somewhat. At later stages, their reduced efficiency is generally more readily apparent and they simply do a "less good" job across the board (Maslach, 1982; Potter, 1980). As mental exhaustion sets in, burnout victims begin to make more frequent errors in their work (Harris, 1984; Matteson and Ivancevich, 1982).

Lowered Standards and Dishonesty

When individuals experiencing burnout develop negative attitudes toward the clients they are supposed to serve, they frequently begin providing a lower level of service, considering it "good enough" for their devalued clients (Maslach, 1982). In addition, burnout has been shown to be reliably correlated with increased employee theft (Jones, 1981).

Obsessiveness

A common response to the increased work demands felt by burned-out individuals is to work harder at everything (Maslach, 1982). In a sort of "overkill" approach, they try to cover all the bases they can, so they don't need to rely on judgment or problem solving. In this way, what is needed is most likely to have been covered somewhere in all that they did. Of course, this comprehensiveness only serves to increase the pace at which physical exhaustion occurs.

Reliance on Rules

As problem-solving skills decrease in the burnout victim and apathy increases, rigid reliance on rules becomes a tempting way to deal with problematic situations. Rules allow one to ignore individual needs and differences, special circumstances, and unique requirements. The burnout victim need not engage in a distressing problem-solving process at all, but can simply treat everyone the same (Muldary, 1983). Librarians who find themselves increasingly "going by the book" may want to investigate their reliance on this mechanism by exploring how they feel about the situations that trigger this response from them. Staleness rather than innovation results from increased reliance on the rules. In addition, risk-taking behaviors significantly decrease, which affects the dynamism of one's work (Ferriero and Powers, 1982; Harris, 1984; Maslach, 1982).

Tardiness, Clock-watching, and Absenteeism

Persons experiencing burnout frequently report a daily struggle against reluctance to go to work. Although the reality of available sick time and concern for maintaining an acceptable facade of good work behavior generally push them toward attendance more than toward absence, victims of burnout have difficulty forcing themselves to get up and get ready for work. As a result, they are frequently tardy (Pines and Aronson, 1988).

When burning-out employees are at work, a significant increase in clock-watching behavior is common (Armstrong, 1978). A concept known as "living for breaks" has been described by Muldary (1983), who reports that persons experiencing burnout have so much difficulty functioning at work that break time is the only time they feel comfortable. They watch for breaks to such an extent that work is viewed only as something to endure until the next break can commence.

Finally, as work becomes less rewarding and sometimes more painful, the burnout victim has less and less desire to engage in it and simply begins to take time off. Absenteeism is one of the most frequently reported work signs of burnout (Ferriero and Powers, 1982; Glicken, 1983; Justice, Gold, and Klein, 1981; Maher, 1983; Matteson and Ivancevich, 1982; Potter, 1980; Stevens and Pfost, 1983; Visotsky and Cramer, 1982).

Workaholism

In early stages of the burnout phenomenon, many victims of career burnout attempt to solve their work problems by working harder—and harder, and harder. As high achievers, they usually have already developed the habit of working long hours or taking work home. As they become less efficient and more stressed, they spend longer and longer hours at work, take more work home, come in on days off, and never catch up. Although they put in more time, their efficiency is so reduced that they don't really get ahead. Instead, they actually need more time to do the same amount of work. When burnout victims attempt to resolve their work problems by workaholic behavior, skipped lunches and delayed or canceled vacations are frequent. Unfortunately, these omissions only serve to increase rather than alleviate their high stress levels (Ferriero and Powers, 1982; Harris, 1984; Visotsky and Cramer, 1982).

Substance Abuse

Many of the monographs on burnout cite increased use of chemical substances as a symptom of burnout (Potter, 1980). However, the relationship between burnout and use of substances such as alcohol or drugs is ambiguous at best, and to date no statistical evidence has been reported to confirm such use specifically as a sign of burnout. There have been suggestions that persons who typically utilize substances to reduce stress levels may be predisposed toward burnout or that substance abuse disorders can run concurrently with burnout, but at present no definitive data are available to lend support to either theory (Muldary, 1983). However, in the literature on stress management use of chemical substances is frequently cited as a nonproductive coping mechanism for stress reduction (nonproductive because it temporarily relieves the symptom by impairing the individual's ability to function productively). The reason substance abuse is included here is that increased consumption of certain substances may be a sign the individual can use to monitor increased stress or psychological needs that have not yet been recognized more directly.

Increases in consumption of alcohol, caffeine, sugar, chocolate, tobacco, illegal drugs, and prescription drugs have been reported by burnout victims (Maher, 1983; Maslach, 1982; Paine, 1984; Pines and Aronson, 1988; Potter, 1987). Use of psychotropic prescription drugs may also commence in early stages of burnout when, as the physical complaints associated with burnout mount, victims seek professional medical care. If the physician is able to detect the probability of an underlying stress disorder, tranquilizers, sleeping pills, or mood elevators may be prescribed.

Behaviors with Serious Consequences

Accidents and near-misses are frequently reported by burnout victims, who may suffer personal injuries from such events (Pines and Aronson, 1988). Suicide attempts and occasional successful suicides have also been reported in the investigation of the burnout phenomenon (Zastrow, 1984).

ORGANIZATIONAL SIGNS OF BURNOUT POTENTIAL

The burnout of individuals can be very costly for organizations, both in terms of the wasted training of burnout victims who leave and in terms of the devastating psychological effect on other employees when the burnout victims remain within the organization (Pines and Aronson, 1988). Sometimes, the characteristics of an organization so promote burnout that it may be risky to be employed within it. There have been suggestions that an entity known as organizational burnout exists, but attempts to define this malady have been somewhat lacking to date. However, certain characteristics of organizations have been identified as conducive to burnout in those who work within them.

Bureaucratization

The number of levels in the organizational structure may have an impact on the amount of stress employees feel. Top-heavy organizations with many managers for few workers are highly likely to produce large numbers of chronic stressors due to conflicting priorities and lack of autonomy at staff levels (Harris, 1984). Glicken (1983) states that the rigid and highly political climate of a multilevel bureaucracy creates certain characteristics in employees, including an exaggerated dependence on rules, aloofness, resistance to change, insistence on their rights of office, and a sense of powerlessness and alienation. In other words, bureaucratic organizations seem to produce employees who demonstrate some of the key characteristics of job burnout. In turn, these employees help create a work environment with a high potential to burn out other employees.

Focus on Competition Instead of Cooperation

Agencies in which competition rather than cooperation is fostered between professionals are also prime candidates for promoting burnout in staff members. The development of a supportive peer network (an excellent way to deal with burnout, discussed in Chapter 6) is effectively sabotaged when there are no rewards for helping each other and when significant rewards such as recognition, promotion, or tenure depend on excelling above the others. In addition, staff members soon learn that asking for support or help may be seen as a sign of weakness and be detrimental to their future career growth (Maslach, 1982).

Increased Conflict

Simendinger and Moore (1985) studied organizational burnout in health care facilities and found that bickering was the most easily discernible and commonly seen characteristic of an organization in trouble. Intraorganizational conflicts ranged from mild differences of opinion to a level that could be characterized as proliferation of major feuds. Sources of conflict were intradepartmental as well as interdepartmental. Simendinger and Moore described management in these organizations as *re*active rather than *pro*active, with a strong emphasis on putting out fires in response to crises rather than planning for the future in order to anticipate and avoid crisis situations.

Sense of Ignominy

When an organization has a large proportion of burned-out and burning-out employees within it, an attitude of resignation or bowing to fate pervades the whole work environment. A sense of lassitude and the inevitability of failure seems to be instilled in all its employees, even those with low potential for burnout. This overall malaise may occur because of external limitations, as when a business suffers significant financial losses but avoids bankruptcy, creating a long-term need for fiscal retrenchment. Alternatively, it may occur through internal activities, as when the organization's leadership retains maximum power while beginning a glide into retirement (Freudenberger and Richelson, 1980).

Whether externally or internally generated, the organization becomes a high-risk work environment for promoting burnout.

Lack of Vision and Stagnation

Organizational complacency also promotes burned-out employees. When the organization's leadership ignores trend indicators from the world outside the organization, ignores competitors, or takes a defensive stance in response to competition, organizational complacency sets in. When the perception that change is to be avoided rather than explored and possibly pursued emerges, it is a strong indicator of organizational lassitude. If complacency and lassitude do not jeopardize its life, the organization may continue in a very static state, neither promoting nor hindering further burnout in employees. On the contrary, a static organization may become a safe haven for people with severe burnout who are in the "deadwood" state, waiting for retirement (Simendinger and Moore, 1985).

Physical Environment

In addition to the physical stressors reviewed earlier in this chapter, some organizations provide physical arrangements that isolate staff members in self-contained work spaces rather than providing for any communal spaces. When lounges, coffee rooms, or employee cafeterias are nonexistent or serve double duty as conference and meeting space, the fraternization that can help employees prevent burnout tends to be minimized (Maslach, 1982).

Psychological Environment

Harris (1984) suggests that organizations in which creative ideas are welcomed are less likely to promote burnout among employees than organizations in which conformity is more highly valued. Most authors suggest that looking at rates of absenteeism, staff turnover, incident reports of on-the-job accidents, and banked vacation time will indicate the emotional health of an organization. When absenteeism, employee resignations, and accidents are high while used vacation time is low, the psychological environment is likely to be unhealthy, and professionals may do well to look elsewhere for long-term employment (Harris, 1984).

Administrative Response

Some organizations encourage a uniform administrative response that promotes burnout. When difficulties consistently arise in the delivery of a service, the objective professional is wise to explore the policies and procedures governing that service. But managers, especially middle managers, are frequently trained to look for problems in the persons providing the service rather than in the service itself. Looking for personal shortcomings such as human error, faulty judgment, or lack of skill is frequently easier than trying to challenge the system by finding shortcomings in institutional operations (Maslach, 1982). Therefore, when burned-out employees seek support from managers, they may hear "Why can't you manage? No one else is complaining" or "What is *your* problem?" In one easy step the institution transfers responsibility to the individual. If (as often happens) the burned-out employees are relatively isolated in their depair by this time, they may not recognize the pattern (and the strength) of their numbers. When multiple staff members are experiencing burnout, it is clearly time to investigate the possibility of a system problem.

Organizations that promote burnout often view employees as a mass rather than as individuals, using coercive policies more than individual reward systems (Simendinger and Moore, 1985). Such insitutions are also likely to value conformance over performance, with an emphasis on doing things right rather than doing the right things. Just as in the case of burned-out individuals who find reliance on the rules a means of dealing with problems, organizations can follow much the same track and, in so doing, increase chronic stress on creative and high-achieving staff members.

SUMMARY

The signs and symptoms of burnout are not exclusive to that phenomenon. On the contrary, they include a wide variety of psychological, physical, and behavioral changes that are commonly recognized as part of the human condition. However, when these changes coexist with chronic work-related stressors and appear en masse and repetitively rather than separately and occasionally, it is time to consider their significance in terms of possible burnout. Individuals can become knowledgeable enough about burnout indicators to halt or reverse the process in its early stages. Recognition of organizational signs of work environments that may promote burnout is also important in order for professionals to weigh the risks of seeking, accepting, or continuing employment in them.

Chapter 4
What Is the Risk for
Librarian Burnout?

In 1981, Sandra Neville reported that the topic of job stress had been given relatively little attention in the literature on librarianship and that what had been written emphasized physical conditions rather than suggesting individual coping strategies. In the intervening decade, a few librarian authors began to pay attention to the idea of burnout in library service work, and a number of articles suggesting the phenomenon of burnout as a potential hazard of librarianship appeared (Bly, 1981; Bold, 1982; Bunge, 1984; Elliott and Smith, 1984; Ferriero and Powers, 1982; Loomba, 1982; Neville, 1981; Patrick, 1984b; Payette and Guay, 1981; Preslan, 1979; Sorenson, 1981; Sullivan, 1982; Todaro, 1982; Walsh, 1982). In addition, data from seven surveys of burnout in librarians were also reported (Haack, Jones, & Roose, 1984; Smith, Birch, and Marchant, 1986; Smith and Nelson, 1983a, 1983b; Smith and Nielsen, 1984; Smith and Wuehler, 1986; Taler, 1984).

ARE LIBRARIANS REALLY AT RISK?

"Library service" is not simply a neat way of describing information work; it carries many connotations that contribute to expectations held for information workers. Patrick (1984b) notes that careers at high risk for burnout are those in which professionals come into direct contact with recipients of services and in which this direct service relationship is characterized by interpersonal intensity, giving, and dependence. There is little doubt in the minds of most librarians that this definition fits library service well. As Elliott and Smith noted in 1984:

The public might think that librarians are hidden away from stress in their book-lined ivory towers. This is a myth that only adds to many librarians' sense of frustration. The truth is that burnout lurks in the shadows of the field of library science as surely as it does in any other.

What is burnout?

Burnout is an overworked, underpaid children's librarian in a busy metropolitan system. Burnout is a reference librarian in a large academic library chronically "bitching" about the demands of ungrateful patrons. Burnout is the habitually late cataloger who watches the clock in morose silence day after day. Burnout is a library director who feels a strong urge to cry each day when forced to defend library policy one more time. Burnout is a school librarian who feels stifled, unappreciated, and pushed all the time. Burnout is "I'd rather be dead than in this job ten years from now." (Elliott and Smith, 1984, pp. 139, 141)

Reference librarians seem most particularly at risk for burnout because of their assignment of general direct availability for an unpredictable stream of requests and demands and their high visibility in most libraries. Charles Bunge (1984), a library school professor who taught reference work, decided to spend a sabbatical year re-experiencing the realities of being behind the reference desk. In part, he sought insight on an observation he had repeatedly made during a number of years of attending conferences and teaching workshops. He had noticed "a rather widespread unhappiness among reference librarians" (p. 128), with feelings ranging from vague dissatisfaction to outright despair, and he wondered about its origins. David Ferriero and Kathleen Powers (1982) and James Rettig (1986) also observed this phenomenon in reference librarians.

Ready identification of librarian burnout as a concept appeared in 1981 and 1982, with a variety of articles by Neville (1981), Bly (1981), Bold (1982), Todaro (1982), and Walsh (1982). These authors were all willing to name the phenomenon as librarian burnout after reviewing the literature on job stress and career burnout, and they suggested a need to address the issue in a widespread manner.

Means that librarians did (or could) use to cope with stress were the emphasis of some of the early journal articles written on the subject of librarian burnout. Preslan (1979) focused on staff turnover issues and librarians leaving their jobs or the profession. Payette and Guay (1981) emphasized sources of stress. Coping strategies for managing stress were the primary interest of Sorenson (1981) and became the emphasis of newly developed workshops and continuing library education courses (Coping with. . . , 1980). Sullivan (1982) explored the anger felt by burning-out librarians and suggested appropriate means for dealing with it.

Altogether, data from seven surveys have been published to date on the question of librarian burnout.

Surveys of Librarian Burnout

Smith and Nelson (1983b) published the results of the first survey in which librarians were polled for burnout symptoms. They asked special librarians to report symptoms of burnout and found that special librarianship may put one at risk for burnout. Yet a companion study of academic reference librarians done by the same authors (Smith and Nelson, 1983a) was published just a few months later and reported conflicting results. The authors used an instrument called the Forbes Burnout Survey for the latter study, an instrument that appears to have been almost entirely eclipsed by the Maslach Burnout Scale and its subsidiary, the Staff Burnout Scale for Health Professionals, which were much more frequently used in later research studies of burnout. In Smith and Nelson's study of academic reference librarians, a mail sample was obtained, and very few respondents reported any of the signs of burnout listed by the Forbes instrument. The authors concluded that burnout may exist but it is not a particular problem among academic reference librarians, and librarians are not especially prone to burnout (Smith and Nelson, 1983a). In a later study of public library reference librarians, Smith worked with Birch and Marchant and found that approximately one-third of the respondents were experiencing some stage of burnout (Smith, Birch, and Marchant, 1986).

Haack, Jones, and Roose (1984) reported the results of a survey of reference librarians taken on site at a conference sponsored by the Continuing Education Committee of the Illinois Association of College and Research Libraries. A total of ninety-two librarians responded, and the results suggested that 42 percent were experiencing some stage of burnout, with 14 percent experiencing severe burnout with severe and sustained psychological tension.

The most comprehensive survey of librarian burnout was conducted by Smith and Wuehler (1986), who obtained 285 responses from librarians in Los Angeles, Salt Lake City, and Canada, as well as library school students at Brigham Young University. The authors used the Maslach Burnout Inventory (1981) and found that roughly 36 percent of their respondents were experiencing the burnout process at the time of the survey.

Izabella Taler (1984) surveyed library directors in New York state to test whether they were observing signs of burnout in their respective staffs. She obtained forty responses with a good cross-section of types and sizes of libraries. Her surprising findings were that 65 percent of the library directors perceived burnout among the members of their library staff and 80 percent reported a need for an effective program to deal with the problem.

Bunge (1987) reported that a 1986 wire service story from England compared the stress level of librarians with that of miners and construction workers. In this comparison, librarians were found to have a low-stress career (2.0 on an undefined scale, as compared with 8.3 for miners and 7.5 for construction workers). Bunge disagreed on the basis of personal observation and experience. To date, most of the studies of librarian burnout also contradict this conclusion.

Common Library Stressors

Librarians have been prey to all of the work-related stressors previously identified as highly correlated with job burnout. In addition, a wide variety of library-specific stressors have been identified in the library literature as well as reported by a variety of librarians in personal communications about what seems to affect them most stressfully at work. The overall list of complaints related to stressful library work conditions bears striking resemblance to overall lists of stressors found when exploring burnout in other professions. The compiled list in Table 2 (page 62) has been split, for easy identification, into two parts, one that overlaps stressors felt by other professionals and one that seems to be specific to the library environment. The correlation between the stressors that seem specific to librarianship and librarian burnout is unknown, but it seems reasonable to suspect that these stressors assist in the evolution of burnout, since studies of stress show that stressors have a cumulative effect. The stressors that are shared with other disciplines were discussed in Chapter 2 on causes of burnout. The librarians' comments related to these library-specific stresses are presented and discussed here.

TABLE 2: Stressors in Burnout	
STRESSORS SHARED WITH OTHER HELPERS	STRESSORS UNIQUE TO THE LIBRARY
Budget cuts Frequent technological changes Increased competition for fewer positions Heavy workloads Bureaucratic inertia Red tape Poor management and supervision Low pay Sex discrimination Obnoxious public/patrons No private space/office Few opportunities to participate in goal setting or decision making Shifting priorities Lack of closure on ongoing projects Few opportunities for advancement Working nights and weekends	Educating away from the librarian stereotype Constant need for speed in response to reference requests Censorship Clerical workload Equipment problems Theft, mutiliation, and destruction of library materials Lack of notice for collection development Emergency duty elsewhere No voice in collection development

Fighting the Stereotype

The complaint about being stereotyped was voiced more frequently by younger librarians than by those who had been in the profession ten or more years. Younger librarians complained that few people understood their library role. Misconceptions ranged from being pitied as an unskilled caretaker of books to being envied as someone who could enjoy the quiet and peace of a roomful of books. Although a high level of intelligence was frequently associated with the popular image of a librarian, significant value to the work was only rarely recognized by members of the public. Surprise at the level of education required for library work was frequently voiced. Librarians noted that even nonlibrarian colleagues, family, friends, and general acquaintances needed to be educated about the realities of librarianship. One school librarian noted that her colleagues resented her because she didn't have a teaching assignment, a job they felt was far more stressful.

Censorship

Nearly every librarian finds efforts to censor the library's collection highly stressful. The librarians who reported this concern noted that the most carefully selected materials could be considered controversial by someone and that censorship issues were not limited to any particular period of time. Materials could be owned for decades before incurring the wrath of a single user or group of users. Most stressful were censorship efforts that were highlighted in the media, those that were ongoing for long periods, or those presented directly to a library board or other governing body without previous notification to the librarians. Librarians felt put on the spot, forced to act as crusaders rallying for freedom of choice whether or not they personally supported the materials in question. They said they felt unfairly attacked because they believed in librarianship as a service to the community and experienced censorship as a statement that they were bringing harm to the community.

Clerical Work

In many libraries, particularly small ones, librarians are regularly required to perform a variety of clerical tasks. A number of librarians found the need to engage in clerical or routine library tasks stressful after working hard to successfully obtain a graduate degree and a professional library position. Although they generally tried not to undervalue clerical work, they felt they had been trained to do more complex and interesting things and resented having to spend time on such tasks. Of course, in many small libraries, such work was inevitable, but even librarians in large research libraries made this complaint.

Equipment Problems

Librarians also cited equipment problems as an irritant that could become a major stressor in certain situations. In particular, audiovisual equipment, photocopiers, and computer hardware were viewed as likely to increase stress when demand was high and breakdowns were frequent. Librarians complained that they were often expected to be technically proficient enough to solve any and all equipment difficulties, from simple maintenance to complex problems. In addition, they noted, users were highly likely to express strong dissatisfaction when the problems could not be readily solved.

Theft, Destruction, or Mutilation of Library Materials

Some librarians reported significant levels of anger over vandalism in the library. School and academic librarians made this complaint much more frequently than public or special librarians.

Lack of Notice for Collection Development

A significant stressor to most public service librarians and library directors was insufficient notice from a parent organization when new programs, projects, or classes were planned that required extensive library support. When needs were expressed at a late date, user demand invariably preceded the library's ability to meet it by a significant time margin. User complaints were frequently increased in this situation, and the librarians reported that their own frustration matched and generally exceeded that of the users. They considered this to be a clear case of a no-win situation that could be avoided if sufficient administrative thought was given to the problem.

Defending against Budget Cuts

Librarians from all types of libraries complained of the difficulties they encountered in budgetary matters. Most stressful was defending the library and protecting its budget when fiscal cuts were required by a parent organization. The librarians noted that it was frequently difficult to overcome the notion that the library, like many other organizations, should generate much of its own revenue. Some reported that the most stressful thing about this situation was knowing all along that they would end up losing no matter how hard they fought. A few librarians saw this situation as a challenge for creative presentation of needs, but this was clearly a minority opinion.

Emergency Duty Elsewhere

School librarians complained of being pulled from the library to do other, nonlibrary work, such as substitute teaching, lunchtime monitoring, or assisting teachers with audiovisual equipment needs. One reported that in the last budget cut she had been required to take on responsibility for her high school's student bookstore in addition to her library functions.

No Voice in Collection Development

Another complaint of some school librarians was that library materials were selected at the school system level without their input. They found themselves unauthorized to select more than a very small percentage of their library collection, and they frequently felt that the general collection provided to them was not the best match for their own students' needs.

STAGE THEORIES OF BURNOUT

The idea that burnout is a process occurring over time and in specific stages assumes that burnout proceeds through some orderly development. Stage theories generally hypothesize that the sequence of the process is relatively fixed but that the rate of change within it may be variable. Cherniss (1980), Edelwich and Brodsky (1980), and Veninga and Spradley (1981) have attempted to identify and describe specific stages that may be found in the burnout process.

Cherniss's Theory

Cherniss (1980) suggests that there are three general stages to the burnout process. The first is impinging job stress, a period in which the individual begins to recognize and identify work-related stressors. Next, the individual generates an emotional response, and in the third stage psychological accommodation is generated.

For example, a librarian may be given multiple assignments with conflicting priorities and unrealistic time frames. Stage 2 is reached when the librarian begins to feel overwhelmed and increasingly experiences anger and anxiety. Psychological accommodation occurs when the librarian decides to just plod along from task to task, letting the overall problem "sort itself out" or, as two of many possible accommodations, decides to change jobs or begins taking anger out on other people outside the work setting.

As a theory, Cherniss's ideas are less well articulated than those of either Edelwich and Brodsky or Veninga and Spradley, and a review of the literature on burnout suggests that they are rarely used to describe the burnout phenomenon.

Edelwich and Brodsky's Theory

The first four of five stages suggested by Edelwich and Brodsky (1980), on the other hand, are heavily used and appear well outlined in many of the journal articles and monographs written about burnout. Edelwich and Brodsky suggested a cyclical process, starting with enthusiasm and followed sequentially by stagnation, frustration, and apathy. A fifth stage, intervention, eventually produces disillusionment.

Stage 1, Enthusiasm, begins the moment an individual enters into a job *if* that entry is accompanied by high hopes and high energy based on unrealistic expectations. If the young worker does not even understand the total scope and responsibilities of the position, unrealistic expectations are inevitable. The authors suggest that the individual may view the job as an ultimate in life's goals and subsequently expend excessive amounts of energy on it. Voluntary overtime is a frequently seen behavioral characteristic of stage 1.

Stage 2, Stagnation, occurs when the thrill of the job no longer eclipses non-work-related pleasures. A renewed emphasis on family, friends, home, and hobbies occurs. In stage 3, Frustration, the value of the job begins to appear doubtful, and limitations within the situation begin to seem stifling or threatening to one's happiness. Apathy, stage 4, sets in when frustration becomes a chronic state but the individual is unwilling or unable to leave the job. In the apathy stage, individuals begin putting in the minimal time required, and begin avoiding challenges and people. It is here,

Edelwich and Brodsky suggest, that the manifestation of emotional, mental, and physical symptoms peaks.

Stage 5, Intervention, is not a chronological stage but a response to any of the other stages; it may even occur in anticipation of one of the other stages. Intervention represents the various attempts an individual may make to halt or reverse the burnout process, including such options as leaving the job, modifying the job description, expanding nonwork interests, or engaging in stress management techniques. If intervention fails to help, disillusionment sets in. When other authors use the Edelwich and Brodsky model, they frequently present it as four stages, with stage 5 labeled as prevention strategies.

Veninga and Spradley's Theory

Veninga and Spradley (1981) also proposed five stages for the burnout process. Their use of popular terminology to label each stage gives their theory some popular appeal. Stage 1 in their theory of burnout, the "honeymoon stage," is essentially the same as Edelwich and Brodsky's stage 1, where enthusiasm, excitement, and energy are high. Subtle differences in the stages begin with stage 2, when Veninga and Spradley say "fuel shortage" begins. At this point, they say early symptoms of job dissatisfaction can be seen in mildly reduced efficiency at work, insomnia, increased use of alcohol or chemical substances, and fatigue.

Stage 3 is one of chronic symptoms that are primarily physical and psychological, with chronic illness, anger, and depression as primary experiences. These authors suggest that a crisis occurs at stage 4, which is actually called the crisis stage. They report that symptoms become acute and obsess the burning-out individual. Stage 5, the epitome of despair, is labeled "hitting the wall" and is described as total professional deterioration and near total dysfunctions in physical and psychological health.

Veninga and Spradley also address prevention and reversal strategies, but their theory doesn't build in the optimism of intervention directly as a stage, which may be one reason it is less appealing despite its use of popular and easily understood terminology.

Accuracy of the Stage Theories

Muldary (1983) suggests that it may be premature to conclude that burnout progresses through an orderly sequence of events and stages at all. He notes that burnout seems to take place in a variety of ways, to proceed at varying rates, and to depend a great deal on the particular unique nature of the relationships individuals have with their total experiential worlds. It seems reasonable and logical to assume that there will be significant individual differences in human responses to job stress, from how it is perceived to the strategies used to cope with it, and, ultimately, to the burnout phenomenon. Nevertheless, the observational data currently available reveal a pattern of similarities in terms of signs and symptoms that suggests that at least some generalizability may be possible.

THE EDELWICH AND BRODSKY STAGES IN LIBRARIAN BURNOUT

As has just been seen, the three major stage theories of the burnout phenomenon reported in the literature each range from three to five stages. The Edelwich and Brodsky stages appear to be most useful in attempting to delineate possible stages in librarian burnout. However, it must be remembered that their suggestions are *only* suggestions and that individual differences and varied life experiences have a significant effect on one's progress (if any) through the burnout phenomenon.

Given a young person who becomes a full-time graduate student of library science immediately after obtaining a baccalaureate, it is likely that stage 1 (Enthusiasm) of librarian burnout would comprise the years of library school and the first professional position following graduation. Stage 2 (Stagnation) would most likely occur after twelve to twenty-four months of on-the-job training and experiencing the real world of work following the theories of library school. According to Rettig (1986), the only library author who places a time frame on it, stage 3 (Frustration) appears to occur after about seven years of library service. Movement from stage 3 to stage 4 (from Frustration to Apathy) is relatively insidious and difficult to pinpoint. Stage 5 (Intervention) is, of course, not coincident with any particular point in time but can be implemented whenever the need for intervention arises.

With this overall outline in mind, a general process of the first four stages of librarian burnout is described in this chapter. Extensive discussion of stage 5 intervention strategies is delayed until Chapter 6, which is preceded by a chapter on monitoring burnout. A heavy emphasis is placed on effective means to monitor potential for burnout, as it appears that early recognition is the most crucial factor in halting or reversing the burnout process. Chapter 5 suggests a wide variety of means for self-monitoring and seeking feedback from others to assist individuals in determining whether or not they are likely candidates for burnout as well as to assist individuals now experiencing the process in its early recognition and treatment.

Stage 1: Library Enthusiasm

Pat looked down at the heavy sheet of ivory-colored paper embossed with the university's seal and proudly read Master of Science in Library Science. A wonderful feeling of pride and accomplishment swelled up inside Pat, readily apparent to all when Pat looked up and grinned with delight at the popping flashbulbs of family and friends. Hearty words of congratulation reinforced the belief that all the best life had to offer was just beginning. A perfect 4.0 average—and boy, that was touch and go a couple of times—it sometimes meant staying up all night to study for exams or finish a term paper. But it was worth it, and Pat could hardly wait for the next step to begin. A new job as Serials Librarian for a public library cooperative program was just the right opportunity, and Pat had fantasies of opening up a whole new world of pleasure to people in several large counties. Serials collections in the local public libraries seemed to need some boosting, and Pat was just the one to do it. Enthusiastic and energetic, Pat expected to do well and make a splash, no matter what it took to do it.

Personal Opportunity

In Stage 1 (Enthusiasm), our hypothetical librarian sees the job of Library Cooperative Serials Librarian as an opportunity to implement knowledge and skills learned in library school as well as a vehicle to "prove" self-worth and improve life for others. In the move from student to professional, the individual experiences a strong drive to do, to help, to get involved, and to become known. When students leave the shelter of the educational environment with degrees in hand, they place themselves in the marketplace as professionals who are now responsible for their own competence and behavior. Logically and naturally, there is an increase in anxiety at this point, in even the most poised and prepared students. To assuage anxiety, the librarian undertakes a comprehensive effort to function responsibly and well in the new professional position.

A strong sense of dedication and commitment is paramount in stage 1, and Pat is likely to spend a lot of personal time on work projects in addition to regular work time. Socialization with other librarians will probably increase, and shop talk will frequently occur at social gatherings. Applications for membership in relevant professional organizations will also increase, accompanied by regular attendance at meetings and conferences. Where possible, Pat will begin to volunteer for opportunities to be involved in organizational activities such as committees and task forces. Again, an extensive amount of personal time will be committed to professional activities.

Job Satisfaction

For most beginning professionals, money and security are only two motivators for work. These individuals are also responsive to intrinsic values such as wanting to make a meaningful contribution to society or finding work to be a stimulating challenge to exercise their skills and abilities. Early in their careers, professionals also meet many of their social needs at work. They identify with and get support from colleagues; they may identify with a parent organization (for example, a university or an industrial leader) and its role in society. Just as each person is unique, so is each person's perception of how satisfying a job is. Personal expectations of high achievers almost always include a desire to feel that their work is significant. Even when jobs are stressful, people who experience a sense of meaning and accomplishment in their work do not burn out (Pines and Aronson, 1988). In illustration, Rooks (1988) describes two reference librarians performing the same tasks in the same library, but deriving job satisfaction very differently on the basis of their individual needs and expectations. One finds satisfaction in the variety of the experience, while the other values opportunity for advancement. The librarian burnout potential of these two librarians will vary with the extent to which their individual values become expectations and how well those expectations are met.

One of the most consistent findings in research on job satisfaction is that job dissatisfaction is highly correlated with increased absenteeism, reduced productivity, reduced mental health, and reduced physical health. The librarian who values variety may become bored if the reference questions are too routine but will be able to tolerate high levels of other types of stress if the questions remain interesting and unusual. The librarian who is seeking advancement may welcome routine questions that give a comfortable sense of competence, a prerequisite for moving upward, but may be highly frustrated by lack of input into administrative decisions.

Reality Shock

The extent to which enthusiastic librarians become candidates for the burnout process depends in part on the extent to which they experience reality shock, which can be defined as the confrontation that occurs between the values, beliefs, and skills of the professional and the prevailing values, beliefs, and skill expectations of the work environment. As the young professional moves into the newly attained position, others' expectations of what is needed and required for the job become clearer, sometimes outlined in formal organizational documents and sometimes offered informally via feedback or suggestions from colleagues and supervisors.

In the case of our hypothetical new Serials Librarian, Pat may entertain fantasies of selecting new serial titles for the region. However, the actual practice may be that a collection development committee composed of librarians from libraries within the region makes selection decisions. Pat's expectation is professional serials selection with a high degree of autonomy; Pat's actual primary responsibility is the efficient implementation of a regional committee's selection decisions, with all the necessary follow-up required to process and organize the serials in various outlying locations. If Pat has included autonomous, thoughtful, and well-received serial selection as a personal criterion, or internal satisfier, for job success, then the actual demands of the job may promote a sense of dissatisfaction or reduced self-esteem. Pat's potential for burnout will increase. If, however, Pat's personal criterion for success is to work well with others in a cooperative effort for a greater goal, there is less discrepancy with the actual practice and demands of the position, less reality shock, and less potential for Pat to burnout.

Bunge (1984) suggests that job dissatisfaction in reference librarians arises from another form of reality shock: the gap between the way reference work *should* be and the way it is day-to-day and question-to-question. He describes this as the gap between the ideal of joy-filled reference work, where each question is perceived as an opportunity to learn more about information resources and the world at large, and reference reality, where the librarian repetitiously provides the same service, learning little in the process, or experiences continuing mismatches between what is known and can be provided and what is desired and needed.

Reality shock can also be enhanced or buffered by the work environment. When newcomers are welcomed and new ideas or recent practice innovations are recognized as valuable input, reality shock is buffered by support and receptivity, even when the new ideas are not fully accepted or implemented. In libraries where tradition is valued above innovation, and new ideas are resisted or discouraged, reality shock can be a much harsher experience.

According to Wilder and Plutchik (1982), professional library school curricula also play a role in the development of unrealistic expectations that contribute to reality shock. These authors suggest that library schools need to present learning experiences that will enhance the individual's understanding of organizations and the nature of bureacracies, to better prepare them for real work settings. They also suggest increased training in interpersonal skills, better preparing new professionals to view work relationships objectively and request clarifications and changes in more effective ways. However, these authors are less supportive of a need to train professionals in better coping strategies for stress management and potential burnout, suggesting that it may not be possible to do this in a classroom setting, or that it might be counterproductive, increasing humanitarian attitudes that would make them more liable for burnout. They suggest that providing trainees with actual stressful situations, through field experiences, simulation, or their graduate education programs, might be a better mechanism for assisting them to cope with uncertainty. Working professionals, however, find stress management workshops extremely helpful in learning practical techniques to be applied to their own situations and do not benefit particularly from the experience of artificially provided stress; it is likely that graduate students would find benefit from a less painful didactic presentation of coping strategies, whether the techniques were applied to a future work opportunity or to their current academic experiences.

Stage 2: Competence and Stagnation

With mixed feelings, Pat reviewed the performance appraisal form one more time. To be sure, there were some awfully good things written there—excellent interpersonal skills, willingness to work hard, eagerness to continue learning, excellent understanding of serials work. That one really said a lot, thought Pat, reflecting back on the naivete and woeful gaps from bibliography and technical processing classes that rapidly emerged in the first few months on the job. And it felt accurate, too, not just good—Pat *had* learned a lot in the last two years. Two years of excellent on-the-job training and a lot of very hard work at home. Even vacations were used for conferences on serials work. Two years of work, thought Pat, that's a long time. . . maybe that's part of the problem—two years with a lot of new ideas and a few major ongoing projects. But not one of them completed. The trouble with serials work was that nothing was static and it seemed to take forever to get things done accurately no matter how good the planning was. Take that one—the one listed as a goal for next year—merge the automated serials list of the public libraries with the one the special librarians in the region had created for themselves. That sounded so easy and compact, like shuffling a deck of cards, almost. But technically, it was a nightmare. And getting the two feuding groups to work together compatibly was even worse. The public librarians seemed to resent the special librarians, who had higher community status and better salaries. And the special librarians just could never get to the same place at the same time for meetings—most of them were in one- or two-person operations with very different demands and downtime hours. Another year to finish that goal? Another five might be more like it! In thinking it over, Pat realized there wasn't really anything wrong with the performance appraisal. What was wrong was not feeling able to take a few days off to lie in the sun, or worrying that joining the little theater group that sounded like such fun would take up too much energy and time.

Pat has moved into stage 2 of librarian burnout. In stage 2, the librarian is capable of (and still is) doing the job at a level consistent with personal and organizational expectations. But a feeling that something is missing has been growing. At this stage, the job is no longer the center of the young professional's life, and work satisfactions alone don't compensate for personal needs that have been set aside. In addition, the librarian emphasizes any absence of concrete evidence of success in the form of a successful product or *measurable* personal accomplishments. Remember how easily Pat overlooked the supervisor's assessment of excellent interpersonal skills in order to focus on the lack of a product in the combined serials list project. This emphasis generates feelings of insignificance, leading the librarian to believe "it doesn't matter what I do."

In stage 2, organizational expectations may also have increased, as the young professional is pressured to perform and perform well. The highly qualified young librarian is recognized as competent and dependable and is expected to continue to perform at peak levels. Time and talent demands may truly become unreasonable. If the librarian can differentiate the reasonable from the unreasonable, there is an opportunity to reverse or halt the burnout process through redefinition and modification of external expectations. Unfortunately, most high achievers have difficulty recognizing demands that are unreasonably great (their own as well as those of others), so they get caught in a cycle of trying to meet demands that are too high.

In librarianship, the continuous expansion of the world of knowledge and the rapid development of increasingly complex technology to organize information so that it is reasonably retrievable remain a constant challenge to the competency of the individual. These same factors present a constant source of potential frustration and can foster a sense of fear, with anxieties ranging from concern that one did not exactly hit the mark in an attempt to match patrons with information to the overwhelming threat of becoming outdated and unable to function at professional levels.

Another facet of librarianship that can prove frustrating for young professionals is that career advancement usually leads further away from the public service responsibilities that initially tempted them into the field. Occasionally, an organization has a career ladder for librarians, allowing them to be recognized for competence without significantly changing their roles within the organization (for example, some academic libraries have librarian career ladders built into faculty status systems). Otherwise, promotion in a library usually means moving into an administrative position of some type. There, the skills and competencies that have been rewarded are generally not those that are now required for additional rewards. Depending on the individual, they may also be less satisfying to pursue or maintain.

Impact of the Work Environment

According to Pines and Aronson (1988), the primary factor in the reversal or continuation of burnout in this stage is the work environment. People who start out with high expectations and high energy, who work in a supportive environment where achievement is rewarded with a sense of accomplishment, who know that they have made significant contributions, who are "rewarded" with increased workloads, who have generally happy and satisfied colleagues, and who can maintain a healthy balance of work and nonwork activities can remain in a positive loop that nourishes and replenishes them rather than burning them out. In work environments where rewards are minimal, stresses are relatively unmodifiable, and inability to make a significant impact is the norm, the potential for individual burnout is high.

Stage 3: Frustration

Pat woke abruptly at the sound of the raucous new alarm clock on the other side of the room and leaped out of bed to shut off the hideous noise. Awful thing! It was necessary though, lately it had been way too easy to sleep through the music on the clock radio or to push the snooze alarm and drop back off to sleep. With a sigh, Pat sat on the edge of the bed and thought about whether to go to work or call in sick. Going in late was always a nuisance. Maybe it would be better just to take another day off. It wouldn't be a lie to call in sick, as the nagging cough from that early spring cold was still hanging on and the alarm clock had precipitated a headache. And it wouldn't really make much difference; everything was a set procedure and the support staff could go on with or without direction very nicely. It seemed to Pat that they were doing that more and more anyway, out of necessity. Pat was taking longer to accomplish less and was cranky with them a lot of the time. Must be getting stale, thought Pat. I just don't get the same kick out of life anymore. Maybe it comes from realizing that, all in all, libraries just don't make as much difference to people as I thought they would, or maybe as I thought I could and used to want to. It's just the same old stuff—same problems, same solutions, same people, day after day. Oh well, Pat yawned, better go make a pot of coffee. I'll need it if I'm going to make it through the day, and I probably have taken too many sick days already this year.

As the reader has undoubtedly guessed by now, Pat is depressed and well into the third stage of burnout, in which reduced work efficiency, increased physical complaints, and questions concerning the value of one's work, and ultimately oneself, abound. The value of library work now seems doubtful, and Pat's early idealism has all but vanished. Not only is there no drive to make a difference, there's no belief that one *can* make a difference. Those early expectations of improving life for the people of several counties, never satisfied, lurk in Pat's unconscious memory as an unfulfilled yearning to make a difference. Instead, work days have a sameness that seems inevitable. Pat is increasingly irritable, a warning sign of growing emotional exhaustion. Pat can't shake a lingering cold, a sign heralding the advent of physical exhaustion. And an early warning sigh of mental exhaustion is evident in Pat's reduced efficiency, requiring more time to do less work. Insidiously, apathy is creeping in: Pat is no longer sure that it's worthwhile to try to do a good job.

Stage 4: Apathy

"Hi, Pat! Haven't seen you for ages—at least several years. How are you? Doing anything exciting? Wish I could stay and chat but I'm on my way to the airport—call me next week and we'll do lunch, ok?" Oh, sure, thought Pat. That ought to be a real treat for both of us. Doing anything exciting? What a joke. All I'm doing is putting in my time. If I had the money, I'd retire and go raise tomato plants for a small farm market. But I don't have the money, so instead I get up at seven, go to work at eight, have coffee at ten and lunch at twelve, followed by coffee at three and leave for home at five or as much earlier as I can manage. Once there, it's just a barrel of laughs to see me throw a frozen dinner in the microwave and settle back to watch TV. Sometimes I wish I had some of the ambition I used to have, but then I remember the hassles of doing extra projects and know I just don't have the patience or the energy to do anything but just wait out the time until I can quit. Maybe if I felt better—I'm always tired and coughing. No, even if I felt better, it's too late.

After ignoring numerous indicators that burnout was progressing, Pat has reached the final stage of discouragement and has emotionally separated from work, which is just a chore to be finished each day before the next day begins. Although many people who reach severe levels of burnout seek relief by leaving a job or leaving a field, others (usually highly motivated by needs for security or realistic financial concerns) remain on the job. Pines and Aronson (1988) call these people, who wait to be told what to do and stifle all complaints through fear that complaining will draw more attention to them, "deadwood." They are generally self-isolated, seeking to avoid rather than to find human contact, eating lunch alone in out-of-the-way places, and arriving and leaving with a minimum of conversation.

Stage 5: Intervention

Stage 5 can be implemented anywhere in the burnout process. For Pat, the pinnacle of emotional, physical, and mental exhaustion has already been reached and ambition is down to zero. Intervention is still possible, and can be explored and implemented now in the same way that it could have been explored and implemented earlier. It just will take a lot longer to work.

First, how did Pat get burned out? To start with, Pat was at high risk: young, idealistic, committed, and perfectionistic. If Pat had looked inward, with a good idea of what to look for, early indicators of a high potential for burnout could have been found in various personal habits and needs. Pat's library school experience already showed a person who wanted and needed to excel, someone who would sacrifice personal comfort and needs to make the desired grade.

How did the work environment contribute to Pat's burnout? In our hypothetical example, Pat's work environment is not presented as particularly problematic; Pat was a high-risk person who could have burned out in any work environment where performance demands were high. But even normal-risk and low-risk professionals can burn out in unusually stressful environments. Looking for the burnout potential of the work environment is also important in preventing job burnout.

BURNOUT QUOTIENT: A MEASURE OF POTENTIAL BURNOUT

Two self-tests have been devised to help individuals measure their risk for job burnout by obtaining two burnout quotient scores. The Personal Burnout Quotient, or PBQ, measures the potential for burnout no matter where an individual chooses to work. The Job Burnout Quotient, or JBQ, measures the potential of a particular work environment to promote job burnout.

Your Burnout Potential

Let's start with you. Pat doesn't really exist, but you do. How vulnerable are you to the burnout phenomenon? The self-test on the facing page has been devised to help you measure your potential for burnout. By taking the test, you will obtain your Personal Burnout Quotient (your PBQ), a score that suggests your level of risk for potential burnout on the basis of your current habits and beliefs.

Personal Burnout Quotient

Using the seven-point scale for each statement, try to rate yourself as honestly as you can on each item. When you are done, add up all your ratings for a total PBQ score.

1	2	3	4	5	6	7
Very Untrue	Usually Untrue	Somewhat Untrue	Equally True and Untrue	Somewhat True	Usually True	Very True

■■

____ 1. I am very singleminded—when I set a goal, I usually accomplish it no matter what.

____ 2. I have trouble thinking when I get upset.

____ 3. My work activities outnumber my leisure activities.

____ 4. My career is extremely important to me.

____ 5. I tend to be perfectionist.

____ 6. I am a risk-taker.

____ 7. I have always considered myself a "Type A" personality.

____ 8. When I have a deadline, I am likely to skip breaks or lunch and work extra hours to get something done.

____ 9. I'm kind of a "workhorse"—I can successfully carry a big workload better than most other people I know.

____ 10. I am a highly organized person.

____ 11. I believe that if you do a thing at all, you should do it well.

____ 12. I find it difficult to relax.

____ 13. I find it difficult to delegate tasks to others.

____ 14. I tend to put things off until the last minute and then work like crazy to get them done.

____ 15. Others consider me an overachiever or think I'm ambitious.

____ 16. I have a history of headache, backache, or frequent colds.

____ 17. I believe library work is very important for the improvement of society.

____ 18. I frequently spend personal time on work activities.

____ 19. It takes me a while to "come down" after an exhilarating event.

____ 20. I am quite competitive, although I may compete more with myself than with others.

_____ **TOTAL PBQ SCORE**

PBQ Interpretation

Score   *Interpretation*

20 - 40   Not at risk for job burnout.

41 - 60   At little risk for job burnout; you would have to work in an environment with a high JBQ for a while before you might have to worry about job burnout.

61 - 100   At normal risk for job burnout; circumstances would be a significant factor to consider. In work environments with a high JBQ, you should watch for signs of early stages of job burnout in order to take appropriate action. In other situations, using a few stress management techniques will help you prevent job burnout. Look closely at the pattern of your responses to the PBQ. If the range is wide, with some ratings of 6 or 7, look specifically at those items. These are the personal characteristics most likely to promote your burnout.

101 - 120   At high risk for job burnout. You should learn stress management techniques and use them regularly. Learn and watch for early signs of job burnout. Avoid working in a work environment with a high JBQ.

121 - 140   At very high risk for job burnout. You should learn stress management techniques and use them regularly; you may wish to seek professional assistance to effect desired lifestyle changes. Learn and watch for early signs of job burnout. Avoid working in a work environment with a high JBQ.

Burnout Potential in Your Work Environment

The Job Burnout Quotient is another self-test designed to help you rate your work environment in terms of how likely it is to promote and enhance burnout rather than inhibit its development. You can use it to rate your current work situation or to look at work sites you are considering for future employment. Remember, if you are experiencing burnout where you work now and are thinking of a job change, it is particularly important to find a new work environment where you can readily implement effective stress management techniques in order to stop and then reverse your burnout.

If you use the JBQ to rate your current work environment, it might be useful to have several colleagues do their own independent ratings as well and compare notes afterward. If the JBQ is high, this can start several of you talking about how to change it. You may just start the type of support group that will be encouraged in Chapter 6 as we explore possible intervention strategies.

If you are using the JBQ to rate a new possible job situation, try to visit the new library unobtrusively to observe and obtain some data before you interview there. When you interview, be sure to request an opportunity to talk with the librarians who will be your peers. Get a tour of the working areas as well as the public areas, and watch people as well as looking at the physical environment. Keep the items listed as part of the JBQ in mind as you go. Immediately after your interview, rate the environment using the JBQ but don't total the final tally; instead, put the rating in a safe place for one week. At the end of that week, rate the library again from the memory of your visit there, without looking at your first rating list. When you have finished, pull out the first rating and tally them both. If they are similar, you can assume they are a reasonably accurate estimate of your perceptions, and you may choose to use the score data to assist in your decision making. If they are widely discrepant, however, look at where they differ the most. Have your perceptions really changed? Why? Are you seeing this library through rosier or rustier glasses now? Notice your feelings about the library, and use your feelings as well as the scoring data when you make your decision.

Job Burnout Quotient

Using the seven-point scale for each statement, try to rate your work environment as honestly as you can on each item. When you are done, add up all your ratings for a total JBQ score.

1	2	3	4	5	6	7
Very Untrue	Usually Untrue	Somewhat Untrue	Equally True and Untrue	Somewhat True	Usually True	Very True

■■■■■■■■■■■■■■■■■■■■■■■■■■■■■■■■■■■■■■■

_____ 1. This library is short-staffed.

_____ 2. Librarians here are not usually consulted when policy changes are needed.

_____ 3. The library budget is insufficient for our needs.

_____ 4. The library collections have not been well developed.

_____ 5. This is a static, not a dynamic, operation.

_____ 6. Librarians here are not paid a good salary.

_____ 7. Librarians here have no private work space.

_____ 8. The librarians here are quite competitive with one another.

_____ 9. The library's overall physical environment is unattractive.

_____ 10. The library's overall physical environment is uncomfortable.

_____ 11. Librarians' offices are unattractive.

_____ 12. Librarians' office furniture is uncomfortable.

_____ 13. The noise level in the library is high.

_____ 14. Lines of authority and responsibility in this library are not clear.

_____ 15. Librarians here have little variability in work assignments.

_____ 16. Librarians here have little autonomy.

_____ 17. Little money is available for regular continuing library education, and requests for conferences are rarely supported.

_____ 18. This is a "traditional" library in most respects.

_____ 19. The long-range goals for this library are not clear.

_____ 20. The criteria for librarians' performance appraisal are not clearly stated.

_____ 21. There is no reward/incentive/merit system here for tangibly acknowledging good work.

1	2	3	4	5	6	7
Very Untrue	Usually Untrue	Somewhat Untrue	Equally True and Untrue	Somewhat True	Usually True	Very True

■■■

—— 22. Communication is indirect and often unwelcome in both upward and downward directions.

—— 23. Librarians here have overlapping responsibilities.

—— 24. Librarians here have to deal with many conflicting priorities.

—— 25. There is no career ladder for librarians in this library.

—— 26. Librarians have to work evenings and weekends in this library.

—— 27. The librarians here do not socialize at lunch or at break times.

—— 28. The librarians here rarely have conversations unless they are talking shop.

—— 29. There has been a lot of turnover in the library staff here.

—— 30. There are two or more higher level positions between mine and the top library administrator.

—— **TOTAL JBQ SCORE**

PBQ Interpretation

Score *Interpretation*

30 - 60 No potential to promote or enhance job burnout. This looks like a terrific, supportive environment. If you have a high or very high PBQ, this is a good place for you.

61 - 90 Has only mild potential to promote or enhance burnout. This environment may be problematic if there is a significant administrative change or if you have a very high PBQ.

91 - 150 Normal potential to promote or enhance burnout; depends a lot on circumstances. It may also depend on you and your specific tolerances. Look at the items you rated 6 or 7 and decide which of them you would find most stressful. If you can employ appropriate stress management techniques to help you prevent job burnout, you may be able to work here comfortably. Be objective in your assessment. If you have a high or very high

PBQ, begin developing support and implementing stress management techniques now. Learn about and watch for early signs of job burnout.

151 - 180   High potential for promoting or enhancing job burnout. Think twice about staying here or moving here. If your PBQ is high or very high, think four or five times about staying here or moving here. This is an important time to establish and maintain good support systems, both personal and professional. You should learn stress management techniques and use them regularly. Learn about and watch for early signs of job burnout.

SUMMARY

With one exception, surveys of librarian burnout to date suggest that this phenomenon is a very real problem for librarians, worthy of attention and concern. Most of the chronic work stressors experienced in the library field are similar to those experienced by other helping professionals. There are also some additional library-specific stressors that can have an impact on active librarians. By using the Edelwich and Brodsky (1980) stages of burnout, it is easy to visualize the progress of a burning-out librarian through stages of enthusiasm, competency, stagnation, frustration, and apathy. Intervention, which will be addressed more comprehensively in Chapter 6, begins with an objective exploration of internal and external factors that place an individual at risk for burnout. As a first step in intervention, two self-tests were developed to measure your vulnerability by rating your personal habits and needs and by rating your work environment in terms of chronic stressors. These two scores, the Personal and Job Burnout Quotients, may help you estimate your need to prevent or reverse burnout.

Chapter 5
Monitoring Burnout: How Close Are You?

The burnout potentials for you and your job are only a part of the picture. If both happen to be low, that's terrific. If one or the other is high or significantly increases without the likelihood of quick respite, it is important to monitor the situation for the beginnings of the burnout process so that preventive efforts can be set into motion. Becoming aware that you are on the burnout track and identifying the stresses that are putting you there are the first steps toward effective coping. This sounds both logical and easy, but it's easier said than done. Most people who have a high burnout potential are competent, self-reliant, determined, and high-achieving individuals who hide their weaknesses well, even from themselves.

PERSONAL INDICATORS

In Chapter 3, it was clear from reported research on burnout that personal signs and symptoms of the process encompass many feeling states, attitudes, and behaviors, as well as somatic complaints. None of them are exclusive to burnout or even to high levels of stress, and most people experience all of them, singly or in combination, at some point in their lives. However, when a repetitive pattern occurs along with significant job dissatisfaction, burnout should be suspected.

Once growing job dissatisfaction is felt, self-monitoring for symptoms of intense stress is the first task in identifying whether the burnout process has begun. If you are already pretty self-analytical, insightful, and self-aware, you may feel you have a bit of an advantage here, as the process of inner exploration may already be habitual. However, signs of burnout can be cunningly insidious; they may already have become so familiar as to feel "normal." In addition, you may find it hard to recognize characteristics you consider weaknesses when you are searching within yourself. It is much more comforting to think of weaknesses as belonging to some other poor soul, someone with whom you can empathize, even sympathize, but with whom you may be loathe to identify. How tempting or comforting it is to overlook weaknesses in yourself is the best clue you can have as to how likely you will be to miss symptoms of your own burnout in early stages.

Getting feedback from others serves to balance the self-monitoring process. If you are missing your own personal symptoms of burnout, they may be suggested in the feedback you get from others. If, on the other hand, you have a tendency to be particularly hard on yourself, you may be unduly sensitive (in a hypochondriacal manner), finding significant symptoms in minute changes, and getting feedback from others can help you put the picture back into perspective. Outside of work, feedback from family and friends is most important, as these are the people who knew you well before and during the period of growing job dissatisfaction. The people you live with will probably be particularly good at identifying which symptoms exist and which don't. People who know you well and who see you regularly but less frequently than those who live with you can serve as good barometers of how much change has occurred over a period of time.

Self-Monitoring

To assist you in self-monitoring, checklists for symptoms of physical, emotional, and mental exhaustion are presented on the following pages. Take the time to read through the practical descriptive section following each checklist, as it is meant to assist you in determining how problematic to consider each of your identified symptoms.

Physical Exhaustion

The signs of physiological arousal in response to stress are generally the first signs you will become aware of, as they are hard to ignore. When your body makes a demand, it tries very hard to get your attention! So the first way way that you can learn to recognize the beginning of burnout is by watching for signs of physiological arousal, the signs indicating that stress (demand) levels have increased. Remember that the longer you have been experiencing chronic stress, the more difficult it is to differentiate these signs without making a special effort, as they may have become so familiar as to almost feel normal for you. The following checklist contains symptoms of physiological arousal that can be used as you begin your self-monitoring task. Check only those that you believe truly describe you as you are right now.

Checklist of Symptoms of Physiological Arousal

_____ I startle very easily.
_____ My sleep pattern has changed.
_____ My eating habits have changed.
_____ I have been gaining/losing weight without trying.
_____ I have a lot of headaches, backaches, or neck aches.
_____ I have been catching cold easily lately.
_____ My allergies are much worse than usual.
_____ I tire more easily.
_____ People keep asking how I feel and telling me I don't look so good.
_____ Sexual activity seems like more trouble than it's worth.

The Startle Response

People under stress startle very easily, as they are literally prepared for "fight or flight" and overreact to sudden or unexpected events. If you don't happen to hear someone coming toward you and he or she abruptly breaks your sense of isolation by speaking to you, do you jump? Does your heart begin to pound hard and your breathing and pulse rate quicken? Does it take you a moment to realize you are safe? Do you put your hand to your chest, sigh in relief, and say to the other person, "You scared me"? If the answers to all or most of these questions are affirmative, you are undoubtedly under stress. All people can be startled by sudden events, but they don't react with the intense signs described above unless they are approaching a state of panic. If the heightened startle response is frequent for you, you are stressed enough to need to do something about it. If the startle response is evident when you are at work but not at other times, the possibility that burnout is beginning is worth exploration.

Sleep Disturbances

Sleep disturbances are another primary sign of stress. A sleep disturbance can be considered any change in your usual sleep pattern. You may begin to have trouble waking up, apparently needing more hours of sleep than usual. If you pop out of bed easily on days off but feel lethargic and too tired to rise on work days, your body may be telling you something about the level of stress you face at work. Even when people don't have trouble sleeping, they are more tired under stress. It takes a lot of energy to maintain a high state of vigilance, which is the body's primary response to the demands of a stressor, and this energy expenditure results in fatigue. For many people, and almost always associated with burnout, chronic stress equals chronic fatigue.

Conversely, some people experience insomnia during burnout. This can take many forms: You may be having difficulty falling asleep at night, waking frequently during the night, or waking up hours early without being able to return to sleep. Some people are more restless during sleep and some have trouble quieting their thoughts enough to attain sleep. Insomnia from stress is less likely than hypersomnia to show as neat a work versus nonwork pattern, so it may be more difficult to recognize work-related stress as the primary problem, unless you have already identified it in other ways.

Another sleep disturbance is a change in dream patterns: You may start to dream more, or more vividly, or you may dream less or have more difficulty remembering your dreams. Many psychologists believe changes in dream patterns are related to the specific stressors a person is experiencing, and some consideration of what you actually dream as well as what you experienced or were thinking of just prior to falling asleep may be helpful to identify your most important sources of stress. You need not be sophisticated in dream analysis techniques to attempt this, as you are looking for associations of ideas, not underlying psychopathology.

Eating Habits

Changes in eating patterns can also signify a response to increased inner tension. As young children, most people learn to equate satisfaction of hunger with warmth, closeness, and caring. In your family, food may be highly associated with celebrations such as holiday get-togethers or birthdays. When inner tensions rise, many people find eating to be a way to ease their tensions and they seek more food at meals or eat more frequently as a result. You may crave chocolate or another specific edible, or you may just feel as if you have the "raging munchies," with a desire to snack on anything you can find. If this happens routinely during or immediately after your work day, it's important to begin looking at exactly what else happens at the time that your hunger is triggered. Do you need a candy bar after each staff meeting? Do you overeat at and after dinner on days when you have had to deal with a lot of problem patrons? Do you do the same thing on days off? Remember, career burnout starts with stresses closely related to work and symptoms that are meant to protect you from those stresses; the symptoms may not generalize to nonwork situations right away.

The opposite change in eating habits can also occur: You may eat less. Sometimes people deal with a rising sense of depression by "punishing" themselves in various ways. In depression, it is not uncommon for people to believe they are themselves to blame for their problems, either by having caused them or by not being competent to eliminate them. What better way to punish yourself than by literally starving yourself? You may unconsciously believe you don't deserve a good meal. Another possibility is that when you are under stress you experience a reaction similar to that of fear. In fear, your body must prepare for other physiological demands than hunger, and your throat may feel "closed" so that you literally can't choke food down it. Or a mild sense of nausea or gastric discomfort may make the thought of eating truly distasteful. Behaviorally, you may find it easy to skip meals or pick at your food, even when facing favorite food items. Try to remember the first time you saw a really scary movie: Did you munch your popcorn faster or set it aside? That will give you an idea of the directionality you will most likely follow if you experience eating changes under stress.

Unsought weight gains and losses often occur in people under stress. If eating is used as a coping strategy, weight gain may occur at a rapid rate. Even conscientious dieters have more difficulty losing weight or maintaining weight loss when they are under stress, as the body produces more adrenalin under stress, which raises the level of blood sugar (Woodman, 1980). The significant weight losses that sometimes occur under stress result when release of thyroxine is increased. This hormone speeds up metabolism, causing calories to be burned more quickly (Morse and Furst, 1982). If you have experienced rapid or dramatic changes in body weight, try to identify the point at which the change began to happen and the point at which it seemed less problematic, slowed, or perhaps even stopped. Once you have these chronological markers, try to remember what else was happening at the same time, especially at work. Did the problem start when the clerical staff were on strike and your spouse was in the hospital for major surgery and three journal articles you had submitted were rejected within days of each other and you discovered your co-director was embezzling funds and you first realized you had been really tired of the "rat race" of library administration for several years? Did it stop when your spouse's medical condition forced you to an early retirement and relocation? This is obviously an extreme example, but it illustrates the process—you are looking for markers that will help you decide if it is/was burnout that you feel/felt.

Aches and Pains

Another physiological response to increased inner tension is an increase in muscle tension throughout the body. Although other muscles may also feel weak or painful, the ones that are particularly susceptible to pain are the muscles of the back and neck. Tension headaches result from tightened muscles at the base of the skull and the back of the neck. Backaches and neck aches are also frequently felt by people under stress. Again, looking for precursors is extremely important. If your aches routinely occur after work but not after leisure activities, your body may be trying to tell you something about how much external tension you are experiencing, and obviously responding to, at work.

Your Immune System

One of the primary results of chronic stress such as that experienced in the burnout process is a change in the body's immune reaction. Theories of how this happens are still being formulated, and the exact mechanism of decreased immunity in times of stress is still being sought (Goldberger and Breznitz, 1982). However, the observable consequences of a reduction in immunity are quite clear, and persons under chronic stress become more susceptible to a wide variety of disorders from the common cold to cancer. Allergies, which are unique sensitivities within an individual's immune system, are particularly responsive to increased or prolonged stress. People under chronic stress often experience heightened allergic reactions and get less relief from usual treatments. If you go from hardly ever needing a sick day to using a lot of them, particularly for minor ailments, look at the worksite to determine its burnout quotient and the effect it may be having on you.

Fatigue

Exhaustion is a key element in the definition of burnout, and it is also one of the symptoms which may appear very early in the process. You may notice fatigue more readily at the beginning of the day when the advent of another long work day appears overwhelming, or at the end of the day when even going home feels like too much required effort. However, it may also appear insidiously during the work day, when you find you are unable to stop yawning while working at a routine task or you consistently gravitate toward furniture on which to sit or lean while talking with others in the course of work. Fatigue from burnout carries over into personal time even into long breaks like vacations. It is important to make extra efforts to gain renewal through rest and relaxation in addition to establishing and maintaining other means to combat burnout.

Your Appearance

Librarians are often surprised, when they think they are handling a difficult situation well, without letting it get to them and without feeling any really troublesome symptoms, to have someone look closely at them one day and say, "You've been looking a little peaked lately. Have you been under the weather?" The external effects of chronic stress may be more readily apparent to others than to the individual experiencing the stress, who may be denying the extent of the problem. Muscle tension is frequently reflected in facial expression, fatigue may produce shadows under the eyes, constriction of blood vessels (as in tension headaches) may result in a paler countenance. One sign that you may be under more stress than you think is having people consistently think you look unwell. If people begin to ask you how you feel with more concern than the usual social civility of greeting, it may be time to begin taking a thorough and objective look for increased or new stressors.

Libido

A decrease in libido also frequently accompanies high levels of stress because the body that must remain alert to danger pushes pleasure into the background. Your level of sexual activity is likely to decline, and promptings in this regard are likely to be less effective than usual. Because of social conventions and concern about job security, satisfaction of sexual needs is likely to occur outside the library workplace rather than within it, so this symptom is one you will probably notice away from the job. However, it is still important to look for work-related stressors as a means of determining whether this symptom is a sign of the burnout process. Are you less interested in sexual stimulation on days when you have been at work? Do you get distracted by thoughts of what has been happening at work when engaging in sexual activity? If your answer to one or both questions is affirmative, you may wish to look for other indications of physical exhaustion.

Emotional Exhaustion

Symptoms of emotional exhaustion also need to be monitored. The next checklist contains emotional symptoms that should be explored as you continue the self-monitoring task.

Checklist of Symptoms of Emotional Exhaustion

_____ I cry easily.

_____ I frequently feel sad without knowing why.

_____ It takes very little these days to get my dander up.

_____ I find people more irritating than I used to.

_____ I argue with others more frequently.

_____ I'm pretty defensive these days and overreacting more.

_____ I wish people would leave me alone.

_____ I'm drinking/smoking/taking pills/eating more without thinking about it.

_____ I feel out of control.

_____ I feel disenchanted with library work.

_____ All I do these days is watch the clock, put in my time, and pick up my check.

_____ I turn down most social invitations and see family and friends less frequently.

_____ Joy feels elusive.

_____ I have a hard time responding appropriately to teasing; I can't seem to laugh at myself any more.

_____ "Small talk" is harder for me than it used to be.

_____ Achieving goals isn't as satisfying as it used to be.

Sadness

Both males and females cry more easily under stress. For many burnout victims, the reason for the need to cry may be elusive; they just experience an overwhelming sense of sadness. Crying is a very specific and appropriate emotional response in which your body attempts to produce relief through the release of tensions. Under usual circumstances, healthy people use tears to express both sadness and joy. In burnout, however, crying does not produce the usual sense of relief and tension release. After the tears, burning-out individuals continue to feel helpless and hopeless, at the mercy of their stressors. When burnout is occurring, the desire to cry is frequently felt at the time and place of the most problematic stresses. You may literally find yourself feeling like crying when one person too many complains that he or she should be allowed to copy tax forms for free because they are government documents or when your only OCLC terminal breaks down for the fifth time in a single day. When the specific trigger is quite minor and your response to it is relatively overwhelming, the levels of overall stress require serious exploration. It is reasonable to grit your teeth and mutter briefly about the dependability of complex technology before figuring out how else to do what you need to do; it is quite another thing to feel as if catastrophe has befallen you and that there is literally no way you can remedy the situation, simply because the terminal is down.

Anger and Irritability

Unreasonable reactions are also reflected in how much anger you feel and show when under stress. Trouble controlling your temper in the face of everyday disappointments and minor work difficulties is another primary sign of burnout. It may take very little aggravation to arouse an anger response, and the expressed anger is likely to be out of proportion to the situation. Frequent eruptions of temper are an additional measure of burnout. When you find yourself snarling at a patron, it's important to figure out why. An increasing sense of loss of autonomy at work can be demonstrated in a loss of control at home. This is one symptom that may, for reasons of job security, be more controlled at work than at home. At work, you may feel just as angry, but you may bite your tongue and remain pleasant, especially in public. It's a different story at home, where you may feel freer to express your feelings or where you may have a greater sense of basic security because the relationships at home usually include a larger emotional component. You may allow a supervisor to reprimand you without reprisal or even to terminate your employment without giving much of a fight. But if your spouse enacts the parallel behaviors of punishing you without reprisal or terminating your relationship, you will probably protest vehemently. There are many reasons home relationships sometimes deteriorate, but if the deterioration of your personal relationship coincides with a feeling that work is overwhelming, it is worth looking at job burnout as a possible cause.

In this same vein, burnout victims frequently find other people quite irritating, even when they are not acting any differently than usual. The difference is in the burning-out individual, who has less tolerance and patience as inner stresses rise. This time the resultant behavior almost always occurs at work, in the form of a progressive isolation. First, you begin avoiding the one certain person who seems most irritating, like the senior reference librarian who seems to love the work and is never at a loss for a helpful response. If you felt better about yourself and the work you were doing, this senior librarian could become a mentor. If you are burning out, the same person may seem threatening. So avoidance feels comforting: maybe you can't change the situation, but at least you don't have to watch it in action. Then you begin to broaden the avoidance pattern to a few more people, like everyone who seems to (most irritatingly) be impressed with that senior librarian and "therefore" relatively unimpressed with you, no matter how hard you try. Remember, you are looking at the situation from the perspective of burnout, that is, cynically. Your logic is more likely to be suspect than accurate. When a colleague compliments the senior librarian in your hearing, it doesn't mean he or she is unimpressed with you—this is an illogical conclusion generated by the process of burnout. However, if you buy into the illogical conclusion, it only makes sense to protect yourself by avoiding the people who compliment the senior librarian as well as avoiding the senior librarian directly. And since it's not really possible to predict who might compliment this terrific senior librarian, the only really safe thing to do is to avoid everybody.

Librarians who are burning out begin seeking peace from irritation by immersing themselves in isolation. The increased need for isolation in order to be away from irritation is also manifested in a desire for physical and emotional distance from others as a means of decreasing possible stressors. You reason that if people would only leave you alone, they couldn't increase the already high demands on your time and talents. A common plea of people experiencing more stress than they can tolerate is to "just be left alone." If you find yourself repeating this plea often (even just to yourself), and realize you are eating lunch alone (maybe in your office or another isolated or private spot), taking the farthermost corner seat at group meetings, looking down or away to avoid eye contact when passing others, timing your arrivals and departures so you don't run into colleagues on the way to and from work, and taking every opportunity to work on projects with as little interpersonal interaction as possible, it is time to review the overall library situation in which you work. For some reason (usually many), your job is not only not meeting your needs, it is actually harmful to your well-being.

Increased arguments are a logical consequence of burnout, as the victims of the phenomenon feel angrier and those with whom they interact object to their anger, defensiveness, or avoidance. Burnout victims frequently even argue with strangers—they don't like the way the service station attendant cleaned their car windows or they are intolerant of service delays at fast-food counters or grocery store checkout lines. Even quiet, well-socialized people may growl at the person in an express grocery line who has two or three items too many to be eligible for that line. Every little infraction of the rules or lapse of competence seems too much to bear and becomes food for conflict or expressed disapproval. In a library, where many procedures and some rules are necessary in order to ensure efficient retrieval of information from the collection, arguments may ensue over requests for deviation from standard procedure or over apparent breaking of rules.

Use of Chemical Substances

Although there are some questions about the directionality of the correlation between increased use of substances and burnout, their coexistence is too common to dismiss. When people begin using alcohol, tobacco, or other substances more, turning to them with less specific thought, the possibility of burnout should be explored. Increased use of substances includes use of prescription drugs, especially those prescribed for treatment of pain. Only you know what your usual habits are in regard to using the varied substances with which human civilization abounds. If you smoke and find more need for cigarette breaks at work, both in terms of higher frequency and stronger desire, if you use alcohol socially and begin "needing" a drink at lunch to get through the day, if your use of prescription pain killers increases, or if you find illegal substances increasingly necessary to relax at night or to get you going in the morning, it is wise to take note of these changes and review your job situation again.

Loss of Control

A very common feeling in the burnout phenomenon is the sense of being out of control, unable to help oneself or anyone else, incapable of changing events or the consequences of them, and feeling trapped in a job with no hope of escape. Every library job will have some parts a specific individual likes better than others, and most librarians select their particular jobs on the basis of the balance between the things they like about the job and the things they don't like. When the balance becomes more negative than positive, the healthy librarian considers changing the job in some way or changing jobs and doing something new. The burning-out librarian is less able to see these options and feels helpless to change the situation in any way. The result is a feeling of being trapped. This naturally leads to a great desire to escape, but since escape is "impossible," the only alternative left is to endure until it finally ends. In psychological terms, this is a classic case of learned helplessness; in work terms, it results in a library staff member who has become "deadwood," relatively unproductive, certainly unprogressive—in short, a detriment to the library operation.

Disenchantment

Burnout victims in other helping professions experience a growing cynicism toward the ultimate value of helping people. In burning-out librarians, a sense of disenchantment with library work may also develop. Daily routines seem unchallenging and the lure of continuing education palls. People feel stale or used up. What was once the mission of educating the public about librarians becomes the drudgery of fighting the library stereotype one more time. Librarians may give evasive answers to social questions related to career in order to avoid having to respond to the suddenly-very-old misconceptions of what a librarian is or does. Introducing little ones to the pleasures of imagination and creative thought in the written word begins to feel like too little too late in a losing battle with television and video games. A "why bother?" attitude grows until it permeates every effort.

Social Skills

As burning-out individuals become progressively more emotionally exhausted, social interaction becomes a trying task. Engaging in "small talk" is more difficult, genuine interest in others is reduced, and the sense of humor that can make life fun becomes frayed. Social invitations are turned down, and burnout victims see family and friends less frequently. They may feel distant and isolated even with a lot of others around or in the midst of a gay party. Teasing is difficult to tolerate, as nothing in their lives seems amusing.

Dissatisfaction

Perhaps most difficult to describe, and yet a pervasive experience in those who have reported on how burnout feels when it is happening, is the loss of true joyousness. Even major accomplishments can leave the burning-out individual with a sense of anticlimax, a sort of "Is that all there is?" feeling. Satisfaction becomes a thing of the past, and life, particularly work life, becomes a chore.

Mental Exhaustion

Symptoms of mental exhaustion are the last area for self-monitoring. The next checklist contains cognitive dysfunctions that are also correlated with burnout and thus may be useful to explore as you continue the self-monitoring task.

Checklist of Symptoms of Mental Exhaustion

_____ I get distracted easily these days.

_____ I am having trouble maintaining my concentration.

_____ I seem to be forgetting things (appointments, deadlines) a lot.

_____ I blank out on names of people I know, even some I know well.

_____ It seems like every time I get ready to go anywhere I have to go back once or twice for things I left behind.

_____ I'm beginning to have trouble knowing what day or time it is.

_____ A lot of times I forget where I'm going and end up somewhere else.

_____ I rely more heavily on rules than I used to, rarely making exceptions even when it would be sensible to do so.

_____ My time management skills seem to be a thing of the past.

Attention and Concentration

Attention and concentration skills are very vulnerable to the burnout syndrome. The abilities to notice and observe (pay attention to) widely divergent stimuli and to mentally manipulate information in a purposeful manner in order to make decisions, draw conclusions, or solve problems (concentration) are skills humans use throughout their lifetimes in order to understand and do complex things. Even in early development, it is clear that some people have the capacity to maintain attention longer than others. There are also individual differences in how well people can be selectively attentive, tuning in to some things and tuning out others simultaneously. A healthy librarian attending a conference in a hotel room with constant low-level air conditioner noise will quickly attend to the presentation more closely and accommodate to the air flow noise, essentially ignoring it unless it changes. Even when very complex information is presented that must be applied in new ways, the healthy librarian can concentrate on the task while never losing the accommodation made to the low-level noise. But burnout victims experience a significant reduction in such attention and concentration skills. Sounds, sights, and even extraneous thoughts get in their way. They may have difficulty paying attention, or they may find themselves attending to unimportant stimuli in preference to what they need. For them, the air conditioning noise may become a primary focus of attention—it is undemanding in cognitive terms, while attention to the presentation and concentration on a learning task are highly demanding. New cognitive demands are interpreted as new stressors, and people already experiencing chronic stress just plain can't handle, and don't need, any more.

On the job, if you are experiencing burnout, you may find it difficult to stay awake in staff meetings. You may have trouble staying with a task long enough to complete it and have trouble finding where you were when you do get back to it. You probably can't attend to two things at once any more, such as looking over selection materials while serving on the reference desk. When you try, you make little progress and escalate your feelings of inadequacy, helplessness, and hopelessness.

Memory

Memory is also highly vulnerable to burnout. Victims of the burnout phenomenon report that anything, from the most mundane to the most important, becomes a candidate for a blank spot in memory. Appointments, details, deadlines, other people's names, and personal paraphernalia are easily forgotten. This may increase stress through concern over forgetfulness, or it may increase stress over the relevance of the consequences of each particular memory loss. In burnout both stresses frequently increase, and burnout victims not only forget things, but they often castigate themselves each time they do so.

For librarians, memory lapses can be particularly disturbing. Even though everyone knows that information is well beyond the capacity of an individual to organize and retrieve without assistance, high-demand processes and materials are frequently mediated by memory. No matter how user-friendly a database is, people remember varied codes and commands for the most efficient use of the system rather than calling for online help or using a lot of written reminders. Sociologically, users express positive appreciation for, and frequently exhibit mild awe at, the librarian's efficient use of memory skills to assist them in complex information retrieval. "How can you remember all this?" they are asked, and the implicit message is that this is an enviable feat. When memory fails, it is not only inconvenient, it makes the librarian feel incompetent. When memory lapses are specific to work events, such as forgetting appointments on the job or leaving things home that are needed at work, the probability of job-related stress is high. When memory lapses occur in both work and personal environments, the possibility of burnout needs to be explored. If memory lapses are generalized to all aspects of life and are pervasive, other psychological or neuropsychological reasons for memory lapses need to be investigated.

Disorientation

In severe burnout, actual disorientation can be experienced. The most basic measure of mental status—orientation to person, place, and time—can be temporarily disrupted. Burnout victims may lose track of time, not just of its passing, but of its logical progression, so that they are uncertain what day or approximate time it is. Logistical confusion also occurs, with people apparently losing track of where they intended to go and ending up somewhere else. Driving to a well-known local restaurant for a library organization meeting, the severely burned-out librarian could literally become confused about where the restaurant is and what is the best way to get there. There have been reports of fugue states in severe burnout, when individuals literally lose whole days without knowing where or how they were spent, without being aware of themselves during that time.

Decision Making

When decision making becomes more difficult, the temptation to rely heavily on rules that do not require additional thought (and may not require any at all) increases dramatically. Circulation librarians cite policies pertaining to borrower eligibility instead of listening to the unique circumstances and needs of an on-site patron. Requests to remove a seldom-used reference item from the library at closing time for return the following day at opening time may be summarily denied without thought by the burning-out librarian, while an exception may just as quickly be approved by the librarian experiencing less stress.

Time Management

Time management and organizational skills are crucial in nearly every aspect of librarianship, where conflicting demands constantly impinge on priorities and where work assignments are often fraught with appropriate but varying occurrences of patron demand. The people most prone to burnout are those who are highly skilled and competent to start with, displaying an ability to respond readily to multiple pressing needs. With increasing job-related stress, these skills deteriorate, and it takes longer to do the same thing. As with memory lapses, a decrease in organizational efficiency can threaten the librarian's career identity and may be extremely difficult to tolerate. Burning-out librarians find it difficult to finish anything, and as new needs are expressed, the pile of uncompleted work simply grows bigger until it is perceived as mountainous. No sense of closure can occur until the work is completed or removed. If completed, the sense of accomplishment that ought to accompany the achievement is frequently insufficient to balance the discouragement that is already paramount. If removed, a sense of failure and a reinforcement of feelings of helplessness results. Either way, burnout is nurtured and the situation feels more desperate rather than better.

FEEDBACK FROM OTHERS

Burnout is often accompanied by an inability to see the forest for the trees. When individual stressors feel overwhelming, the individual begins a form of crisis management, dealing with each new detail as it occurs rather than looking at the overall situation. If stressors increase insidiously rather than dramatically, this is even more likely. Any librarian whose library burned down one day would have an emotional response to this overwhelming stressor: What will happen now? Can it be rebuilt? Where will the money come from? How can the irreplaceable ever be replaced? Will I have a job during the rebuilding? Will I ever feel safe here again? Reactions to a catastrophe can include nearly all the symptoms of burnout in totally healthy librarians who have reasonable questions and show appropriately concerned responses to the situation. They could be shocked, depressed, or angry, feel sick, and have trouble remembering things or keeping their mind on what they are saying. And they wouldn't need anyone to tell them where all that stuff was coming from—they would know: "I haven't gotten over the shock of the fire yet." And that's the difference. Burnout is *not* the result of a single major stressor; it occurs gradually, sneaking up in the form of a bunch of little stressors that build up and don't go away. And sometimes, the burnout victim is in the middle of it without seeing it. That is why it helps if someone else, someone outside the process, can suggest what may be happening and start the sufferer thinking about self-monitoring. Otherwise, the suffering continues and no steps are taken to alleviate it.

Feedback from Family and Friends

If you are burning out, those closest to you in your personal life are the people most likely to notice the changes in you and to associate these changes with work-related stress. As these people share your personal environment, they are in a terrific position to notice that things are not really much different outside of work. Ergo: If you're showing signs of stress and the stress isn't in your personal life, it's probably at work. It's an easy connection to make. Unfortunately, it may not be so easy for you to hear. When people who are important to you say you're different or are acting different, especially when the differences are reflected in negative rather than positive terms, it can sound and feel like criticism. If you're already stressed from work, this helpful feedback can easily become just one more stressor. Not only do you feel helpless to change what's happening at work, but now you see yourself as a helpless pawn under the control of work stress who can't even function normally at home. And when you don't like the message, you may be tempted to discount the messenger. Burnout prevention, however, requires outside feedback as well as personal monitoring in order to see the whole picture. Indeed, for many librarians, the suggestion from family and friends that something seems to be building up at work may be the first impetus to suspect burnout and explore it as a possibility.

The following is a list of complaints you may have heard from those closest to you. If they hit home as you go through the list, ask yourself, answering as honestly and objectively as you can, whether they are accurate representations of how you have been behaving outside of work.

Checklist of Complaints from Family and Friends

_____ You bring work home a lot more than you ever used to.

_____ You never seem to want to go out any more.

_____ You seem preoccupied all the time.

_____ Your temper is really short these days.

_____ You're so defensive.

_____ You never seem to want a little romance or sex.

_____ Work seems more important to you than anything else.

_____ You need a vacation and you won't take one.

_____ You seem to think the library can't run without you.

_____ You never seem to have enough time for fun things.

_____ You used to like to garden, work on community projects, etc. Now, you don't like to do any of that.

_____ You're smoking/drinking/eating more than you used to.

_____ You're really a restless sleeper lately.

_____ You look tired all the time.

_____ You get sick an awful lot lately.

Feedback from Supervisors, Colleagues, Subordinates, and Patrons

Individual burnout is equally evident to the people you work with, and they, too, may see the process more readily than you do from your position at its center. According to Pines and Aronson (1988),

> people's burnout is almost never a secret from their colleagues; if people are burning out, whether or not they know it, others around them are quite aware of it.

When there is a disparity between your perceptions and those of your colleagues in terms of your functioning, it is important to look at the situation. When a supervisor, colleague, subordinate, or patron makes an effort to give you feedback from their perspective on how your behaviors are differing from their expectations of you, it is useful to step back and try to view the situation rationally and calmly. Have you really changed? Are the changes things you like? Remember, people tend to have adverse reactions to all change, whether positive or negative. You may have been making an effort to become more assertive, and the complaints you are currently receiving are related to this change, which you like, purposefully implemented, and want to maintain. Or are the complaints related to a change you were unaware of making? Has the new assertive you already become familiar and people are noticing that you now frequently go beyond assertiveness and behave aggressively? Another important consideration is whether the expectations these others have of you are reasonable and realistic. If they are, and you are significantly deviating from them, then your behavior may need self-investigation.

The following checklist contains complaints about your work performance that you may hear from supervisors, colleagues, subordinates, or patrons. Again, your task is to check off those you hear frequently and then review them as honestly and objectively as you can, deciding which of them are an accurate representation of you.

Checklist of Complaints at Work

_____ You frequently leave early or come in late or both.

_____ You act unmotivated.

_____ You no longer volunteer for anything.

_____ You seem to avoid colleagues and peers.

_____ You prefer to work alone rather than with someone else even though you used to seem to enjoy working with others.

_____ You seem to avoid library patrons, especially the ones who are likely to cause irritation. And when you can't avoid them, you're not as patient with them as you used to be.

_____ You take long lunch breaks.

_____ You refuse to have lunch with others. When asked, you say that you're going to skip it and work through lunchtime or that you'll eat something hastily in your office so you can get back to work.

_____ Paperwork takes you longer than it used to.

_____ You don't get into personal conversations much any more.

_____ You don't get as much work done as you used to.

_____ There are more complaints about your work than there ever used to be.

_____ There are more complaints about your attitude than there ever used to be.

_____ Your absences have increased.

_____ You seem preoccupied all the time.

_____ You don't meet deadlines any more.

_____ You give the library a bad image.

SUMMARY

You are the only person who can really decide whether you are burning out. To explore this possibility, you need feedback from other people in addition to extensive self-monitoring for the signs and symptoms of burnout. Looking at yourself through others' eyes as well as your own helps you keep the picture in a realistic perspective as well as providing you with additional data to consider. Paying attention to the content of complaints you get at home and at work (rather than getting defensive about them) can be very enlightening. If you discover you're already on the burnout track, remember that burnout is stoppable and reversible. If you're not burning out yet but have a high PBQ or work in a high-risk environment, remember that burnout is also preventable. The key is to notice it's happening or about to happen.

Chapter 6
Individual Coping: What Can You Do About Burnout?

Individual differences are especially relevant to coping strategies for stress reduction, as each person is unique in terms of what works effectively to reduce chronic stress, what needs are unsatisfied during times of stress, what problematic beliefs are triggered by stress experiences, and what may enhance rather than reduce stress. For example, many people find hypnosis a useful technique and learn to self-initiate a trance state. For people with strong control and autonomy needs, the process of learning hypnosis by giving themselves into the temporary "control" of another as they learn is itself too stress provoking to be useful. Visotsky and Cramer (1982) report that any one stress management technique will work for only 30 percent of the population.

According to Caplan (1964), effective coping has seven general requirements, and the ability to utilize coping strategies that will work for you depends on how well your techniques meet these requirements. First, a coping strategy should allow an active exploration of the realities of the situation, rather than a submerging of reality. Techniques that are aimed at merely reducing the symptoms will help you reverse or halt burnout only if they are used to bring you to a point where you can tolerate scrutinizing the situation realistically. Second, coping requires the ability to tolerate conscious recognition of your feelings. You cannot cope with feelings of anger if they are repressed and expressed only as passive-aggressive behaviors that you yourself do not recognize as hostile. The third criterion for effective coping is an active effort to engage the help of others, a recognition that seeking help expands your potential resources rather than indicating personal failure. Fourth, effective coping requires that problems be broken down into manageable parts to be worked through one at a time. A librarian who says "My job is so upsetting I don't know what to do" can only really begin to cope with the problem when it is specifically, even concretely, identified through exploring the aspects of the job that are distressing. Fifth, effective coping requires an awareness of symptoms and their exhausting effect so that resources can be used well to gain appropriate control over specific aspects of the job. The sixth requirement is to recognize what one can control and what is beyond one's control. Finally, in order to cope effectively, an individual must have a fundamental self-trust and a trust in others. This trust serves to generate and increase a sense of optimism that something can be done to bring about a positive outcome.

These seven criteria can be useful when selecting the most effective means of coping in times of unusual stress (like the example in Chapter 5 of a library burning down) or in early stages of burnout when resources are still relatively intact. At later stages of burnout, any means of coping, even those that satisfy few of Caplan's criteria, may be temporarily useful to help the individual deal with the terrible strain of the burnout phenomenon. Later, after some relief is found, less effective coping strategies can be replaced with more effective ones.

It has been said that there only three things that can be done about stress. The first is to eliminate it. The second is to try to reduce it. The third is to accept that it cannot be changed and change yourself instead so that you can tolerate it better.

STRESS ELIMINATION TECHNIQUES

The elimination of some stressors is perhaps the best means of reducing overall levels of stress. In the work environment, it is likely that fewer stressors will be under your direct control in terms of elimination than in your personal life. Nonetheless, there are some ways of taking direct action to eliminate the stressors that are within your province.

Taking Direct Action

Waiting for stressors to go away by themselves is a fruitless endeavor unless the conditions that produced them go through substantial changes. Stress elimination thus requires direct action.

Rarely does the burning-out individual have the authority to eliminate workplace stress through personal action, so direct efforts to eliminate stress usually involve leaving it behind. Changing libraries or changing jobs within the same library are two possible means to eliminate stress. Eliminating stress by directly enlisting the assistance of a person or group that does have more authority to affect the work environment is a third alternative.

Changing Jobs

Changing jobs may mean taking a different position within the same organization, moving to a new organization, or leaving the field entirely. These can all be effective means of elminating the job stresses that helped to generate your experience of burnout, but unless you become sophisticated at identifying potential risks and means to avoid them, you simply increase the number of jobs in which you repeatedly burn out. When you quit in desperation, you are less likely to make a wise decision on the next job you accept, and you could literally change jobs without changing your stress level at all. Changing jobs without changing your unrealistic expectations (the ones that set you up for burnout to start with) also can lead to disaster, as the next job, no matter how good, will probably not help you meet unrealistic expectations. Quitting your job to take on a new one then becomes associated with a continuing sense of failure rather than a successful recognition of a means to eliminate stress. However, sometimes it is important to recognize an environment as unhealthy for you, and because choosing to change jobs enhances your sense of control, this should not be ruled out as an option. If implemented, it should be implemented in tandem with investigation of environmental potential to promote burnout (the JBQ discussed in Chapter 4) and with self-monitoring measures (found in Chapter 5) as well as the other stress reduction techniques presented in this chapter so that the burnout process can be recognizied and interrupted or reversed if it seems to be continuing in your new work environment.

Enlisting Help

Managers in work environments with a high potential to promote job burnout are themselves at risk, so they may be very responsive to suggestions of means to eliminate some stressors. In a chronic short-staffing situation, for example, they may be willing to consider eliminating some services or delegating some traditionally professional-level tasks to competent lower-level staff members. They may be willing to relieve you of responsibility for some tasks or agree to modify your job to eliminate some stressors. Ask! If the answer is negative, your situation is no worse than before, and if the answer is affirmative, you have gained some relief. Even a negative answer has a usefulness, for it allows you to bring attention to the problem and to express your concerns and needs.

STRESS REDUCTION TECHNIQUES

Stress reduction is the next best thing to elimination of stressors. Techniques for reducing stress serve to reduce the impact of the stressors by changing the workplace demands. Specific stressors in the work environment that cannot be eliminated by direct action may yet be reduced through taking action. Setting realistic goals, confronting others, and setting limits by saying no may assist you to reduce some workplace stressors. Other actions, such as learning relaxation techniques, taking time out from work, building a support system, and improving the physical work environment, can help as well.

Setting Goals

Setting realistic goals for job performance rather than striving for abstract ideals may help you to reduce stress. If your goal is to make the world a better place, it is easy to question whether your role in maintaining the best clipping file within your school library's entire school system satisfies your goal. And when goals are consistently unmet, no matter what the reason, a sense of futility emerges. If your goal is more *concrete, specific, measurable,* and *realistic,* such as preparing students to do appropriate research by maintaining a clipping file that will meet fourth-grade students' information needs 65 percent of the time, the question of whether you met your goal is answerable. Such a goal is less prone to generate unwanted feelings. Burnout is a process in which long-term frustration of highly idealistic goals produces a loss of enthusiasm and idealism. Setting personal priorities on what you want, need, and can attain from work may help you to reappraise goals that are unrealistic and unattainable.

When you have set achieveable, specific, measurable goals, focus on them. Do not develop alternative goals. This will simply leave you feeling unsettled and and divide your energy, which may already be in limited supply. If you get to the point where a goal is not achievable, you can decide on a new goal at that time.

Confronting Others

When the primary sources of work stress are people, direct assertive confrontation may be necessary. If a supervisor provides only negative feedback, for example, a means of reducing stress may be to attempt to gently educate the supervisor through an expression of your feelings and needs. Sensitivity, tact, courtesy, and a willingness to take responsibility for the problem of how the situation affects you (it's *your* problem, even though the supervisor may be a primary factor in causing it) are all required. Many books on assertiveness, including one written exclusively for librarians (Caputo, 1984), are available to assist you in learning effective confrontation techniques.

Saying No

Learn to limit your commitments as a means of reducing your stress. When a demand is unreasonable, say no. Saying no not only keeps you from getting overloaded, but it also lets the other person know you care about yourself and the quality of the job you do, and it reminds you that you have choices and can be in control of the situation. Saying no carries some risk, but if the risk of saying yes is getting overloaded and burned out, saying no may be well worth whatever other consequences could result. If you have trouble saying no, ask yourself this question: "If I never say no, how valuable is my yes?"

Learning Relaxation Techniques

Many techniques for relaxation have been suggested, and scholarly works as well as many popular books and tapes are available to assist you in finding a technique that works for you. These range from spirituality to physical therapy. The emphasis in relaxation training is to slow down. True relaxation results in physiological changes that reverse the increased sympathetic nervous activity aroused by the General Adaptation Syndrome. In a state of true relaxation, metabolism slows, heart rate slows, and breathing slows beyond the point of simple rest, as in sleep or quiet sitting.

Four basic elements are required for all relaxation techniques. You will need a quiet environment, a mental device, a passive attitude, and a comfortable position. A quiet environment is one in which there are as few distractions as possible. Sound, even background noise, may prevent relaxation. Choose as convenient and quiet a place as possible. Mental devices may vary from repeating a single nonword syllable, as in the mantra of transcendental meditation, to using relaxation tapes or imagery. A passive attitude means you should "go with the flow." If you scrutinize your performance you will be working hard at relaxing and find true relaxation impossible to achieve. Finally, a comfortable position is one in which muscular effort is reduced to a bare minimum. If you are sitting, your head and arms should be supported. Tight-fitting clothing and shoes should be removed.

The following are but a few of the many relaxation suggestions that are available commercially and in the literature. If these are not of interest to you, many more can be readily found in a brief information search of this area.

Quick Relaxation Techniques

Quick relaxation methods are brief techniques that are effective and fast, and can be used almost anywhere. Practicing slow breathing while you are waiting on hold on the telephone or sitting in a waiting room is an example of a quick relaxation technique. Closing your eyes for two minutes and concentrating on seeing the color blue is another example. Studies have shown that blue is the most relaxing color for imagery in stress reduction (Potter, 1980). For fun, try some of the following:

> Tense, then slowly relax your dominant hand, paying attention to the difference between tension and no tension.
>
> Close your eyes and imagine a very calm blue sea or sky.
>
> Close your eyes and mentally say a single word over and over again. Choose a word that is symbolic for you, such as "love" or "God." Then try again with a word that is not symbolic, such as "ah" or "now." Say the word in your mind each time you exhale, drawing it out slowly.

Think of a problem that has been bothering you, and imagine yourself writing it on a piece of paper. Fold your imaginary note into a paper airplane and sail it away for now. (This is a good fantasy to use for a brief stress break from an aggravating meeting.)

Close your eyes and imagine the smell of a gardenia or rose.

Touch a piece of smooth wood and stroke it lightly.

Smile at nothing, just to feel your smile.

Close your eyes and imagine the sound of running water in a fountain or a brook.

Fifteen-Minute Relaxation Techniques

The time allotted to a coffee break can be even more profitably used for stress reduction. When devoted to relaxation, fifteen minutes can be a very effective period of time. Here are some techniques that can easily be completed in fifteen minutes.

Pretend you are standing on the holodeck of the newest Star Trek *Enterprise.* Close your eyes and watch the sliding doors open before you. Notice the perfection of the hologram that is reproducing your favorite place. You might be sitting beside a clear mountain lake or walking peacefully through a beautiful forest or lying comfortably on a sandy beach. Listen for the sounds of the birds or the breeze or whatever fits your special place. Try to feel the warmth of sun on your skin and the coolness of the breeze. Notice the colors. Let yourself enjoy the moment to its fullest. Revel in it. Relax. When it's time to go back to work, go back to the door and leave, but remember to store the hologram in the ship's computer so you can go back again.

Shut your office door, stand up and do a short routine of simple stretching exercises. Slowly bend down toward the floor, reaching both arms down to it, and then slowly raise your arms out to your sides and bring them up over your head. Put your hands at your waist and slowly bend from side to side, forward and back. Do standing pushups against the wall by placing your palms flat against it with elbows bent and then slowly pushing away until your arms are straight. Hold onto the back of your chair and rise on your toes, then do a slow deep-knee bend and return to a standing position.

Do the following brief deep-muscle relaxation exercise. Find a quiet place and sit comfortably. Take your shoes off. Tense the muscles of your dominant hand and then relax them, noticing the difference. Think of your hand as heavy and warm. Tense the muscles of your dominant forearm, then relax them, noticing the difference. Think of your hand and forearm as heavy and warm. Tense the muscles of your dominant upper arm and then relax them, noticing the difference. Think of your hand and arm as heavy and warm. Tense the muscles of your other hand and then relax them, noticing the difference. Think of your hand as heavy and warm. Tense the muscles of your other forearm and then relax them, noticing the difference. Think of your hand and forearm as heavy and warm. Tense the muscles of your other upper arm and then relax them, noticing the difference. Think of your hand and arm as heavy and warm. Tense the muscles of your dominant foot and then relax them, noticing the difference. Think of your foot as heavy and warm. Tense the muscles of your dominant lower leg and then relax them, noticing the difference. Think of your foot and lower leg as heavy and warm. Tense the muscles of your dominant upper leg and then relax them, noticing the difference. Think of your foot and leg as heavy and warm. Tense the muscles of your other foot and then relax them, noticing the difference. Think of your foot as heavy and warm. Tense the muscles of your other lower leg and then relax them, noticing the difference. Think of your foot and lower leg as heavy and warm. Tense the muscles of your other upper leg and then relax them, noticing the difference. Think of your foot and leg as heavy and warm. Tense the muscles of your hips and then relax them, noticing the difference. Think of your lower body as heavy and warm. Tense the muscles of your abdomen and then relax them, noticing the difference. Think of yourself as heavy and warm. Tense the muscles of your chest and then relax them, noticing the difference. Think of yourself as heavy and warm. Tense the muscles of your shoulders and then relax them, noticing the difference. Think of yourself as heavy and warm. Tense the muscles of your neck and then relax them, noticing the difference. Think of yourself as heavy and warm. Tense the muscles of your jaw and face and then relax them, noticing the difference. Think of yourself as heavy and warm. Tense the muscles of your forehead and then relax them, noticing the difference. Think of your forehead as cool and calm while the rest of your body is heavy and warm. After practicing this one a few times, try to do it by simply relaxing each muscle group, one at a time, without tensing them first.

Imagine sitting on the grass near a softly flowing river in a park that is nicely landscaped and well tended. You have a soft blanket to sit on, a cool drink, and some bread, cheese, and fruit. It is a warm late spring day, almost summer, but not quite. Butterflies are nearby, and occasionally you can see a fish jump. You can smell newly mown grass. The river makes a soft gurgling sound and there are flowering trees on the other side. They make a delightful contrast to the blue sky, blue-green water, and green grass with their white and pink flowers. A few wispy clouds add some floating white to the sky. Birds sing. Enjoy your picnic lunch before you return to the world of work.

Make up your own pleasant fantasy similar to the one above, with details to stimulate all your senses. Over time, embellish and practice it. The better rehearsed the fantasy is, the easier it will be to call it up when stress is particularly great and you really need it.

Longer Relaxation Techniques

The most well-known technique for deep muscle relaxation was developed by Benson (1975), who sought a way to disengage the sympathetic nervous system through demobilization while simultaneously engaging the parasympathetic nervous system, thus inducing a relaxation of Selye's General Adaptation Syndrome. In Benson's progressive relaxation technique, people are taught to assume a comfortable position and then to systematically concentrate on varied muscle groups, one at a time, inducing and experiencing relaxation. Starting from the toes and moving upward, students of this method learn to produce total physical relaxation. The third fifteen-minute technique presented above is a brief version of the full Benson technique, which takes forty-five to sixty minutes to practice.

A great variety of relaxation tools, including both audiotapes and videotapes are available commercially. Many include subliminal messages for relaxation as well. Try several and experiment with the best times for their use in your personal schedule. Many people prefer to use them just before bedtime as a means of relaxation preparatory for sleep. They can also be used at midday or before specific stressful events such as anticipated confrontations or high-stress meetings.

Another effective technique for achieving deep relaxation is through the practice of biofeedback. Various electronic devices, ranging from simple hand-held temperature or heart rate sensors to more elaborate machines with multiple sensors, are used to assist people in achieving relaxation by learning what to do to change the readout (or tone) provided by the electronic device. Intuitive responses are translated into measurable indicators of the relaxation process as it takes place.

Meditation takes a variety of forms, but each produces deep muscle relaxation. In transcendental meditation, a mantra is repeated as the devotee sits quietly and allows the physical body to relax. In other types of meditation, people consider abstract concepts, such as the sound of one hand clapping, or focus on bodily sensations, generally respiration. It can be very relaxing to practice deep, slow breathing and attend only to inhalations and exhalations.

Hypnotic induction of relaxation can be externally stimulated through a reputable hypnotherapist or can be self-induced. Many books are available on self-hypnosis, and it is possible to learn effective hypnotic techniques in this fashion, although many people find self-hypnosis easier when they have learned it through the guidance of a trained professional.

One final suggestion for lengthier relaxation techniques is bathing. For a relaxing bath, try using water just slightly warmer than lukewarm, scented oil or crystals to soften the water, candlelight, soft music, and a bath pillow. Fill the tub so full body immersion is possible, and let yourself enjoy the sensation.

Breaking Away

The stresses encountered during work can be reduced by arranging for intermittent rest breaks to serve as emotional breathing space.

Time Out

Time out is the opportunity to leave a stressful task or situation temporarily in order to refresh yourself and get ready to tackle it again after a break. You must recognize your need for some time out by monitoring various symptoms of stress. In personal interaction, you may notice your muscles tightening or your breathing quicken. While working on stressful tasks, you may realize you have made more mistakes in the past thirty minutes than in the previous three hours. Whatever the indicators are, taking a respite is likely to help. What you do in the time out can be important, but there's only one criterion to watch for: What you do should reduce your stress rather than increase it. You may choose to get a cup of coffee, collect materials from another location, or look out the window for a few minutes. If you need a longer break, you might take a walk, visit an art gallery, listen to music, play cards, or plan a dinner party. If you're in the middle of personal interaction, you might ask for a moment to think and then shut your eyes. Unless you take more than ninety seconds (which is quite enough time to concentrate on a quick relaxation technique), the other person will be very unlikely to interrupt your concentration. The important thing is to notice as soon as possible when you need a break from work and find a way to give it to yourself.

Making Appointments with Yourself

When your schedule is too hectic and you can't find time for work breaks, make an appointment with yourself. Put it into your appointment calendar, and keep it as you would any other appointment. If necessary, put in a standing appointment—a half hour every Tuesday and Thursday, for example. Giving yourself work breaks is too important to brush aside because pressures are increasing. Use your self-appointment time to nurture yourself and relax.

Decompression

Deep-sea divers enter an environment of high atmospheric pressure when they dive to great depths. If they return to the surface too quickly, they experience a very painful and potentially harmful condition caused by the release of nitrogen bubbles into the bloodstream. To avoid this condition, known as the bends, divers make short stops at various depths on their way back to the surface, making a gradual transition in a process known as decompression. In a similar way, people working in high-stress environments may find it useful to decompress before returning to the normal pressure of their personal life. Maslach (1982), who developed this concept as one technique in the treatment of burnout, defines decompression as "some activity that (a) occurs between one's working and non-working times, and (b) allows one to unwind, relax, and leave the job behind before getting fully involved with family and friends" (p. 102).

The specific decompression activities you choose must be selected to suit your particular needs and may vary from listening to headset music on the subway ride home to taking a solitary walk in the park for ten minutes before leaving for home. Or you might make an agreement with your family that the first ten minutes home are always and irrevocably yours to relax in the hot tub, walk around the garden, or put your feet up while you read the newspaper, after which you will feel like a normal person again and will join them.

Mental Health Days

Some organizations recognize mental health days as a legitimate use of accrued sick time. Even if your library does not explicitly or implicitly do so, you are free to use sick days for this type of preventive health care just as you might use them for visits to physicians' offices or to an outpatient clinic for diagnostic testing. A mental health day is taken when you feel so stressed that you need the relief of spending an entire day doing things to help yourself feel better. You might spend it watching old movies, visiting an exotic restaurant, fishing, getting a massage, shopping, hiking, visiting museums, or going to a concert or matinee theater performance. Again, the primary criterion for an effective mental health day is that you use it in a way that rejuvenates you rather than in a way that increases your stress. If you use it for shopping, for instance, you should not have specific goals such as getting half your Christmas shopping completed or finding the antique lamp you've been searching for; instead you should have relatively vague goals such as looking around and buying Christmas gifts if any strike your fancy, or antiquing for fun and seeing it as a bonus if you find the perfect lamp.

Compartmentalize Work Activities

If you can leave work problems at work rather than living with them twenty-four hours a day, you will reduce your stress level immensely. Of course, there are professions that require you to be on call even when on your own time, but, in general, librarians do not have to respond to a lot of off-work-time interruptions or emergencies. Setting realistic goals for how much work can be done in a day or a week will assist you in not feeling pressured to keep working at home. There is a genuine sense of freedom in walking away from work on a Friday sans briefcase, planning not to worry about work issues again until Monday morning. Making agreements with colleagues not to talk shop at lunch is another way to compartmentalize work time and allow break time to be a viable opportunity to help you feel refreshed. Setting short-term goals for long-term projects compartmentalizes the work into mini-accomplishments that sustain you in working toward the final goal.

Vacations

Burnout victims often have huge amounts of accrued vacation time although their sick time may be depleted. The reason is simple: They frequently succumb to the maladies of burnout and require sick time but seldom can convince themselves to take a vacation, because there is "too much to do" or "too much happening right now." But postponing vacations is unwise. Long breaks from work, which offer a true respite because you do not take work along and do not think about it while you're away, are necessary for the rejuvenation of your physical health and the rekindling of your emotional well-being. A realistic dilemma is having to work extra hard before you can go on vacation and finding a huge pile of work waiting for you when you return. If possible, try to get work coverage while you are gone—someone who can attend to all routine matters in your absence, saving only necessary items for you. Spend the time you normally spend getting ready to go in training this person to take over for you. An added benefit is that each time this person assists you he or she will get better at it and you will not have to be overwhelmed each time you return.

Building a Support System

Even if you have a stable and supportive network of family and friends, work-related social contacts are essential to deal with job burnout. Research suggests that good work relationships have a positive effect on job satisfaction and one's general sense of well-being, while poor relationships increase worksite stress (Argyris, 1964; Cooper, 1973; Cooper and Marshall, 1976). If you work in a small library, this may mean developing strong relationships with professionals from other disciplines within the same organization as well as with librarians from other organizations. A support system at work helps buffer stress by providing resources for empathy in difficult situations, assistance in problem solving, and opportunities to achieve a sense of competence by providing this same support to others.

Pines and Aronson (1988) list basic ways in which professional support systems help. First, they provide technical support by giving you access to people who understand the complexities of your work and can brainstorm technical problems with you. They also provide emotional support by giving you access to people at work on whom you can count when you need to talk about the frustrations you are feeling. Support systems provide you with some technical challenge as well, when you are called on to help colleagues with problem-solving or brainstorming activities. Of course, they can also provide emotional challenge, as you are asked to give emotional support to colleagues. This allows you to practice good stress management. Finally, Pines and Aronson say that professional support systems are one of the best sources of people who will listen respectfully to you and provide a basis for social reality in the workplace.

Discussions with peers help put failures in perspective and allow you to realistically balance frustrations and successes. Burn-out victims find it easy to ignore their successes and focus heavily on failures; a good peer support group challenges this focus. It also provides professional companionship with others who share common stressful and rewarding features of the work and workplace. It gives you informed shoulders to lean on, which may be helpful in suggesting solutions to problems or recommendations of ways to cope with them. It lets you know you're not the only one with the problem. Even when there is no solution, sometimes just having that recognized and shared is helpful. Peer support increases personal as well as professional insight when you are open to what you hear, and it gives you more opportunities to help others and feel competent. It allows you to feel comfortable with having negative feelings about your work by finding out that others also have these feelings without becoming ineffective or considering themselves bad.

A good support group at work has another positive aspect: It helps you see the funny side of problems. The patron who was your personal last straw today may have interacted with Sandy last week and with Val the week before. As you compare notes, you may begin to see the patron as a source of entertaining stories you can share with each other instead of the bane of your existence. Does this mean you are laughing at or poking fun at someone? Yes, in the same way that comedians and cartoonists help us see the funny side of human behavior. Personally laughing at the patron is rude and inappropriate. Laughing about your feelings and perceptions by describing the patron's behavior and your reaction to your peers is a means of coping. Lazarus (1979) describes finding humor in a situation as emotion-focused coping and suggests that this is a highly effective strategy for dealing with stresses over which you have no control. Elliott and Smith (1984) suggest that keeping a diary of "wacky things patrons say and do" is one way to combat librarian burnout.

How to Gain Allies

To build a professional support system if your library doesn't have one, you'll have to take a few risks. You will need to express your feelings openly and you may have to ask directly for support. When you get it, acknowledge it ("Thanks for your support, it means a lot to me"), and reinforce the positive value of it for both of you ("I really appreciate your help; we got a lot more done by working together on this"). Let colleagues know when you sincerely think they've done a good job on something. Giving positive feedback will help them keep from burning out, too. Be helpful. Socialize at lunch and break times. Take an interest in the nonwork activities of others. Give information freely about your own nonwork interests. To build a support network, you need to start seeing your peers as likable people—as friends, not merely as colleagues.

How to Lose Allies

Support is so important in the prevention and treatment of burnout that the last thing you want to do is to lose potential allies. However, there are some things that can get in the way of professional support networking. If competition between group members is great and there are significant differences in resources, status, or perceived power or real power among members of the group, chances are stress will be enhanced rather than reduced (Carrilio and Eisenberg, 1984). Hierarchical reporting status may also affect the situation; it is more rare than common for managers and subordinates to provide reciprocal support of the kind discussed above. When colleagues use social interaction time for nonproductive complaints (a "bitch session" with no solutions offered or sought), or for individual confrontation that ought to be conducted privately, stress increases rather then decreases. Another tendency that can have the opposite of the desired effect is for someone to catastrophize, that is, *help* you worry by bringing up all kinds of problematic possibilities that you hadn't thought of yourself.

Improving the Environment

The physical dimensions of the work environment include space, architectural structure, noise, and the ability to personalize fixed features to meet individual needs. Although there may be environmental factors well beyond your control or restrictive policies that prohibit personalization (you can always challenge these through assertive requests), the environment has such a major effect on the amount of work stress that it is important to make it as stress reducing as possible.

Privacy and Community

Ferriero and Powers (1982) believe that private work space is essential for reference librarians who work long hours in public locations. The availability of communal space is equally important for librarians who work in varied technical service or administrative capacities that require relative isolation for long periods. Both types of space need to be available, attractive, and comfortable.

Noise

The psychological definition of noise is sound that is unwanted by the listener because it is unpleasant, bothersome, disruptive, or believed to be psychologically harmful. Noise is stressful, even when it is in the background in the form of ignorable "white noise," such as the air conditioning sound mentioned earlier in an example of stimulus accommodation (Chapter 2). Sound conditioning for offices, use of soft music to mask other sounds, and reduction of equipment sounds through judiciously chosen locations (photocopiers placed together in a separate room) or noise enclosures (on typewriters and printers) may assist in reducing stressful noise. Plants, draperies, carpeting, and textile wall hangings have all been found to help reduce environmental noise (Rader, 1981), and these may be obtainable items in your library.

Light and Color

Overhead fluorescent lighting is extremely stressful, despite its effectiveness in providing sufficient light for work to be conducted. For private spaces, investing in a few inexpensive table or floor lamps to provide a softer atmosphere with indirect light is tremendously helpful for stress reduction. The atmosphere becomes comfortable, even "homey," despite the presence of desks, computers, and other work items. Color is also important. Blue has been found to be the most restful color, but all the soft pastels are soothing. Bright colors are certainly attractive in many areas, but they heighten stimulation and demand a response from the body. To reduce stress, put softer colors in high-demand work areas.

Personalizations

Personal touches also add a sense of comfort in a stressful work environment. A favorite art print, pictures of significant people in your life, and desk accessories that match your particular style, whether modern or traditional, are all the kinds of things that can create a more restful environment for you.

STRESS TOLERANCE

When you are in a work situation where chronic job stress is encountered but the reality of your life situation is that you really do need the job, viable alternatives are not readily available, and you cannot change the level of stress in the work environment, another means of dealing with it is required. Changing yourself is one way to increase your ability to tolerate a bad situation until such time as you can leave it. We have already seen attempts to change in reviewing behavioral symptoms of burnout: The use of withdrawal and isolation is one of the best illustrations. In order to deal with burnout, some people change themselves from outgoing interested and interesting individuals into hermit-like persons. Of course, this change only exacerbates the problem. Other more productive changes can help you deal with stress effectively without exacerbation.

Taking Good Emotional Care of Yourself

Emotional exhaustion is the hallmark of burnout victims, who need to take particular care to reduce the emotional drain of dealing with work-related stressors. The suggestions that follow all relate to ways in which individuals can make themselves less prone to burnout even when chronic stressors are inevitable.

Take Things Less Personally

Reframing is a psychological technique that helps you place a stated problem in a new perspective. In dealing with the burnout process, it is important to recognize that work stressors are largely situational—only their effect is personal. When you reframe, you change the perspective from "What's wrong with me?" to "What's wrong with the environment?" The sense of relief found in burnout victims when they no longer think of themselves as inadequate for not being able to cope better with truly impossible situations is gigantic.

Become More Assertive

Relationship skills can help you reduce tension in the work environment by helping you make more positive, win-win contacts with other people. Assertive communication is an effective way to express your preferences and needs and to work toward resolving conflicts. Taking appropriate assertive action, even if the result isn't what you hoped it would be, helps maintain your self-esteem because you know that you did the best you could to try to get the results you wanted.

Reframe Beliefs

Zastrow (1984) suggests that "burnout is caused by experiences that people encounter and by what people tell themselves about these experiences" (p. 145). As examples, he notes that people give themselves self-defeating messages such as "I've had it" "There's no use trying," or "I give up." If these are reframed, burnout victims have a better chance of overcoming their burnout experience. Instead of telling yourself how bad a situation is, try to see a positive aspect in it. An impossibly heavy workload gives you a wealth of experience in a short period of time. Role ambiguity allows you to formulate your own role and design the job to your liking. Role conflict gives you an opportunity to see how parts of the overall picture fit together. At the least, working where all these burnout causes exist gives you a golden opportunity to learn what to avoid in your next work environment.

Reframing is particularly useful if you have a tendency toward perfectionism, a characteristic that launches you toward burnout. Everyone make mistakes, and mistakes are wonderful one-trial learning experiences. They teach you what doesn't work so that you can look at the situation again, analyze why the first idea didn't work, and try a new idea. You learn a lot more by making mistakes and rethinking a problem than by accidentally getting the correct solution the first time through. When you think of mistakes as failures rather than as learning experiences that give you more data than accidental successes, making mistakes can add to your stress level. Reframing them as positive learning experiences helps reduce your stress.

If you are (or, through burning out, have become) a chronic helpless thinker who first sees and thinks "I can't" before considering the possibility that you can, try to consciously change these automatic thoughts. Thought-stopping is a specific technique that may be useful if you have trouble getting rid of unwanted thoughts. When an unwanted thought pops into your mind, mentally yell "Stop!" and reframe the thought to a positive one.

When you feel compelled to do something that you know will increase your workload and your stress level, ask yourself why you're thinking "I should" or "I ought" rather than "I could," and remember that you are making a choice with every acquiescence to an internal "should" or "ought" message. It is just as important to choose to take care of yourself when you are burning out as it is to choose to meet internal or external demands for tangible performance.

Develop a Healthy Perspective

A healthy perspective recognizes that the world is imperfect and that life is often unfair. More important, it is a recognition that *all* people have problems with everyday living. Laugh and play. Enjoy what you do, take pleasure in what goes on around you, and look for the things that give you satisfaction, pleasure, or pride. Listen to jokes and tell some of your own. Have fun with life.

Pray

For many people, prayer serves as a very effective stress reduction technique. Psychologically, prayer allows you to give the problems to a higher authority, one that is beneficently inclined to help you. Physically, prayer has been used to evoke a relaxation response by many practitioners of a wide variety of religions and sects for many centuries. Even the earliest recorded religious works suggest that a union with a higher power is not possible unless all distractions, all physical activity, all worldly things, and all thoughts are eliminated so that a higher level of consciousness can be obtained: This is the relaxation response in a spiritual form (Benson, 1975).

Compliment Yourself

Give yourself deserved pats on the back when you do a good job on something. Positive feedback at work is so important that a lack of it is considered a causative factor in burnout. If it is generally absent in your organization, you can encourage confirmation of your worth and seek some positive feedback by telling your supervisor, "I think I did a good job on that." At the same time, you give yourself a little boost. On the way home from work, focus on something good that happened or that you did and give yourself a pat on the back. If it was truly a rotten day, reminisce about some of your most memorable compliments—the ones that really meant, and still mean, a lot to you. Enjoy the memory, and don't dilute it by comparing it to any other time, including now.

Keep a Journal

A personal journal helps you to express your feelings in a private way and also gives you a nice record to track actual progress and patterns of stress. It can be easy to get bogged down in problems when you are a burnout victim, and having a record of the good times as well may assist you in keeping your spirits up. Chronic stressors are sometimes difficult to define, and a journal may also help you see patterns that you may miss in the need to respond to continuous crises.

Check Off Your Tasks

Making daily "to do" lists is frequently recommended in time management training. In burnout, such lists can provide some positive reinforcement if they are used appropriately. Making a list of separate small tasks for a project that feels overwhelming allows you to see some progress and feel a sense of accomplishment as each task is completed.

Be a Participant

Isolation nurtures burnout and allows the process to continue. Socialize, and get involved with other people in a variety of ways. You might try volunteer work for an organization you like. Attend the talent performances of people you know—the neighbor child in *Rumplestiltskin* or your sister's vocal recital. Go along on group excursions, even if you don't want to be particularly active. Getting involved is easier to do in early stages of burnout than in later stages, but can be useful as you reverse the process and begin feeling physically up to more activity.

Seek Professional Help

For severe burnout, the assistance of a professional to help you sort out underlying beliefs and provide ongoing support as you seek to halt and reverse the burnout process may be helpful. Stress management workshops, group therapy, and individual psychotherapy are all available resources that might be of help.

Taking Good Physical Care of Yourself

Physical exhaustion is also a primary aspect of the burnout phenomenon, making good preventive health practices a necessity for those who work in stress-inducing environments. The suggestions that follow are basic ways in which you can take good care of your health and reduce the impact of chronic work-related stress.

Exercise

Physical exercise is one of the best coping strategies there is. Working out tensions by jogging, cycling, playing tennis, skiing, doing aerobic exercises, or riding an exercycle in your living room serves to revitalize you and fights depression at the same time. A particularly rigorous program is not as important as the regularity of the program. Physical activity gives you something other than work to concentrate on, which frequently allows you to solve work problems unconsciously, finding more effective solutions after the exercise break than you could have come up with by skipping it.

One of the most difficult problems in engaging in regular exercise is that we see it in terms of needs. It can take a lot of energy or preparation to get ready for many of these activities, which may require special equipment, special clothing, or a special location. It's hard to play racquetball in your office. We also tend to worry about the time it takes to get ready, get cleaned up afterward, and, of course, engage in the activity itself. Quick and easy ways to get regular exercise include taking fifteen-minute walks at lunchtime, doing stretching exercises in the morning before you dress, making regular dates to meet others for shared activities, and jogging at night just before bedtime. The point here is not what you should do or how you should do it, but making a commitment to do something regularly.

It's particularly important to be realistic about exercise. Seeking medical advice prior to starting a rigorous program may be wise if you're deconditioned by a long lapse from exercising. Warming-up and warming-down techniques are also recommended. It is better to start out an exercise program slowly in the beginning and revise it upward than to overdo it and cause yourself harm.

Eat Well

Nutrition is also important in stress management. Eat regularly and moderately and pay attention to dietary restrictions related to specific health conditions. If you have been advised by your personal physician to maintain a low-salt or low-cholesterol diet, for example, stick with it. Feeling guilty about your eating habits adds to your stress level rather than reducing it. Eating at regular meal times and following the body's natural metabolic pattern (humans burn more calories in the morning than at night) are also important.

Nutritional habits that have been found to be most highly correlated with stress include eating from vending machines, eating "on the run," eating while you work, and skipping meals for lack of time (Leighton and Roye, 1984), so try to avoid these habits. It is important to look for patterns in your own eating habits to determine when you are more likely to demonstrate poor, rather than good, nutritional behavior. You might keep a diet diary for a while, jotting down what you ate, when and where you ate it, and how you felt at the time. That way you can discover what effect your mood has on your food intake.

Specific recommendations for diet include limiting or eliminating alcohol, caffeine, and sugar from your diet. High intake of caffeine (over 700 milligrams. daily, or more than five or six cups of brewed coffee) can produce pharmacological actions that are indistinguishable from those produced by high levels of anxiety (Morse and Furst, 1982).

Simplify Physical Demands

If you hate housework, hire someone to clean for you on a regular basis. If mowing the lawn gets you down, do the same. Allow yourself to not do things that were somehow drilled into your self-identity as part of a work ethic.

Expanding and Growing

A way to retrieve your multidimensional self from the flatness of burnout is by seeking ways to rescue old interests and seek new ones that allow you to take a broader satisfaction in life and human culture. From taking a new perspective on certain work responsibilities to learning new things, setting personal priorities and goals may help you achieve a healthy balance betwen work and personal satisfactions.

Do the Same Thing Differently

The pervasive sense of helplessness that is felt by burning-out individuals can be conquered through making choices that help you feel back in control of the situation instead of feeling controlled by the situation. By making small choices, even just choosing to answer the phone differently or greeting more patrons as they come in the library, you build your belief that you *can* make effective choices. Then, when you need to consider larger issues, such as the impact of budget cuts or staff shortages, you will feel more able to cope. Go to workshops and conferences on topics relevant to your daily work. They can also help you see new solutions to chronic problems, or teach you new skills that lessen the impact of chronic problems.

Do the same things differently in small ways too. Vary your routines and change tasks when they begin to drag. Use blue highlighters instead of yellow or orange (remember, blue is more relaxing). Move the pictures in your office around. Answer the phone differently. Be creative and try new approaches; people are artists as well as technicians, so let your artistic soul out.

Do Something You Used to Enjoy

Pick up a violin or a paintbrush and palette again, start singing in a community group, or take up the birdwatching you once enjoyed as a scout. Think back on the best times of your life, whenever those were, and remember the things you enjoyed doing for fun. Make time for them once again. It may be helpful to find others who once shared the same interest and work at renewing your skills together.

Do New Things

Go to workshops and take continuing library education courses that are not directly related to your everyday work as a means of enhancing your professional skills. Start something brand new that you always wanted to do but never had time for, or that you never even thought about doing until the current opportunity came along. Learn to fly, take a wine-tasting class, get involved in a sports program, or read the great classics of literature. Take a community adult education course for fun.

SUMMARY

Dealing effectively with burnout depends on your ability to recognize the problem, take responsibility for doing something about it, identify specific major strategies for coping (i.e., eliminating, reducing, or adjusting to), and develop a variety of productive coping skills that can be mobilized as needed. There is no single most effective antidote or prophylactic for the burnout phenomenon. No speedy cure is available. There are no miracle drugs for it. It takes work (just what the burnout victims are least likely to desire) and energy (what they are least likely to have) to cope with it. But coping, stopping, reversing, and even preventing burnout are all possible. In severe burnout, coping may be harder to manage and may take longer to have an effect but, just as water eventually wears away stone, a commitment to practicing effective coping strategies will have a positive effect. You will immediately feel better just because you are doing something to help yourself. It might take a little longer for significant positive effects to happen at work, or in your physical condition, depending on how burned out you are, but if you stick with your treatment plan you will eventually feel a lot better. The treatment of choice for burnout is just that: choice. You have choices to make in determining useful changes in your lifestyle and workplace. Most important, you have the opportunity to make the choice to seek to overcome burnout. Everyone, including burnout victims, has a wealth of stress management techniques hidden away in conscious and unconscious memories that have served them well over a lifetime of temporary stress-provoking situations. Mobilizing these and learning others is the best way to deal with the chronic job-related stress of burnout.

Chapter 7
Organizational Coping: What Can the Library Manager Do to Prevent Burnout?

A variety of organizational characteristics have been identified that correlate well with low staff burnout. Managerial leadership that provides emotional support, administrative structure, and open information is one important characteristic. Explicit rules and policies, coupled with opportunities for staff to be self-sufficient and to participate in decision making, are also likely to decrease potential for burnout. Support of peer networking and an emphasis on creativity and innovation are also helpful. Possibly most important, awareness and management of environmental stressors, from physical factors to workload pressures, is required (Shapiro, 1982).

The organizational costs of burnout are high. Lost motivation, increased staff turnover, poor delivery of services, increased employee theft, increased tardiness, and greater absenteeism all result in significant indirect cost to organizations. Direct costs include employee health care costs for diagnosis and treatment of burnout. No one has been able to calculate the actual cost of stress in American organizations, but it has been estimated to be in excess of 100 billion dollars annually (Matteson and Ivancevich, 1982; Minnehan and Paine, 1982). In addition, the presence of even one staff member who is significantly suffering from burnout has an adverse effect on the organization, as one highly discouraged person can have a stronger effect on morale than one or more highly positive people (Harris, 1984). Thus, organizations have a high stake in trying to prevent burnout, and many administrators are beginning to recognize this need. According to Maslach (1982), burnout is a function of bad situations in which once idealistic people must work. If burnout is to be prevented and reversed, these bad work situations must be changed so that they promote well-being rather than sabotage it.

Sandra Neville (1981) also supports organizational coping as an effective means of dealing with librarian burnout:

> Professional librarians responsible for the direct-service functions are frequently faced with the occupational hazards of job stress and burnout, which are nonproductive outcomes of organizational shifts in priorities. Training the individual to develop personal strategies to cope with stress by improving management skills will provide a temporary reprieve from certain aspects of job frustration, but a review of organizational design can offer more permanent solutions to a problem that taxes both the individual and the institution.
>
> Library organizations and professional associations can create environments that will help or hinder effectiveness, facilitate or inhibit service activities. Libraries in the next decade must recognize the shift from a materials orientation to a client orientation and design the organization structure to serve the work flow of library services. Associations and other professional groups must address the direct-service functions as a cohesive activity deserving more than fragmented attention. Only then will nonproductive, stressful conditions contributing to services-staff frustration and burnout be changed to productive conditions in an organization environment supporting direct-service responsibilities and objectives.

REALISTIC JOB EXPECTATIONS

People who are burned out and working in a bureaucracy like a library may have some difficulty differentiating the things that can be changed from the things that cannot be readily changed (Maslach, 1982). The library manager can assist in this discrimination by clarifying the current structure of work roles, service goals, and evaluation criteria. Opportunities for professional staff input should be clearly identified, and such input should be positively reinforced when offered. Informal expectations should be comfortably explored, and those that are unrealistic should be gently confronted and modified.

Breaking Down Problems

Library managers can help their professional staff members to prevent and reverse burnout by breaking global projects down into finite pieces that neither overwhelm the staff member nor suggest lack of confidence in the individual's capabilities. Librarians who are burning out may no longer have the capacity to do this for themselves because of mental exhaustion, and they may not have the emotional resources to request assistance because of emotional exhaustion. It is up to the manager to observe staff members for signs of burnout and offer assistance when needed. It must be remembered, however, that for librarians who are *not* experiencing burnout, this assistance decreases their personal autonomy and may be more detrimental than helpful.

Orienting the New Professional

A common practice in new employee orientation efforts is to have the new employees spend a lot of individual time at the beginning of their employment with the other staff members with whom they are most likely to be interacting and working. After a period ranging from hours to weeks of this sort of semi-involvement, the new professionals are expected to begin handling a full workload. The idea is to give the new professionals an overview that will serve as a foundation and then let them jump into the pond and swim as well as they can. One or more persons might be assigned to be available for questions "as they arise," but often the new employee is expected to suddenly fit into the system after this orientation exposure.

Unfortunately, the nature of such individual orientation plans is that current staff members provide information (usually much more than can be absorbed) that they think the new person will need, and the new person, who can't yet know what is actually needed, doesn't know how to sort out the truly useful from the not so useful. In addition, information overload is soon reached, and later portions of the orientation process may not even be heard. The library manager and current staff expect the new professional to remember and be competent with all the information that was provided, and the new staff member feels incompetent if this is not possible (and, of course, it isn't). Both parties start out with unrealistic expectations, and the road leads downhill from there.

A more realistic approach to orientation helps set a standard of realistic goals. New staff members need to build up to a full workload and a full knowledge of the system more gradually and more interactively. Alternating actual tasks with orientation sessions allows this to happen in a more effective way. Encouraging a realistic assessment of what can be done in a particular period of time and of the level of expertise required at various staff levels or for various assignments is extremely important as well.

CLEAR LINES OF AUTHORITY AND RESPONSIBILITY

The hierarchical organization of a library is not always as clear as that of a for-profit organization, particularly when the library is part of a greater parental structure such as a university, hospital, company, or school. The advisory role of nonprofessional groups such as Friends groups and library committees is not always clearly defined, and the greater the superstructure of the organization (as in a large university), the more difficult it may be to determine where the authority of a library administrator, let alone that of a staff librarian, begins and ends. However, because it is clear that role ambiguity is an important factor in increasing burnout, defining the hierarchical reporting structure clearly is extremely important. In this regard, if the staff librarian has more than two or three levels of management to deal with in order to gain approvals for requests and needs, there will be little perception of managerial interest in staff needs.

Organizations that promote the development of librarian burnout may not have sufficient follow-up and backup systems. A follow-up system is a check that assigned tasks have been completed on time and as requested. A backup system is an emergency plan to keep primary services operating in times of unusual difficulties. Most libraries have some sort of backup plan, although the emphasis may be on the physical environment. There are generally plans for what to do if lights or other electrical systems fail and plans for filling in staff shortages caused by unplanned absences. However, formal follow-up plans are relatively scarce. A regular system can be a brief monthly or quarterly progress sheet listing current goals and the level of accomplishment to date. When goals are clearly out of reach, unrealistic expectations can be identified. When progress is slow or inhibited by other factors, support and resource assistance may be offered.

Nature of Supervision

One of the most important facets of the hierarchical organization is the nature of the relationship between library managers and the other members of the professional staff who report to them. Quality supervision entails precision-tuned social skills and the ability to communicate clearly and directly in a nonthreatening manner to provide effective positive feedback, to notice potential for accomplishment and potential for discouragement, and to troubleshoot performance problems before they arise. Both the overly critical supervisor and the one who seems to be running for the most popular vote are likely to be problematic for their subordinates and are also likely to generate a burnout-prone environment. Supervisors who see themselves as trainers or coaches have the best success in counteracting burnout, as they encourage individual growth and development and open the door for group applications of theoretical knowledge to practical situations.

If there is a single most important facet to the effective supervisory relationship in terms of burnout prevention, it is probably a high level of mutual trust. When librarians and their managers know they can express feelings and identify problems safely, without incurring sanctions, they can work better together to solve problems and deal with feelings that get aroused. Rooks (1988) suggests that there is a tendency in some libraries to create an atmosphere of one big happy family. Unfortunately, as numerous studies of family dynamics show, negative feelings can be viewed as threatening to the family structure. Libraries that encourage a parent-child trust relationship ("I'll be here to take care of you") rather than an adult-adult trust interaction ("We'll work this out together") promote, rather than prevent, burnout.

JOB MODIFICATION AND ROTATION

Job enrichment programs in industry were developed on the assumption that jobs should include opportunities for personal achievement, recognition, growth, responsibility, and advancement (Muldary, 1983). If all jobs were sufficiently enriched, there might not be any burnout-prone organizations. But since not all jobs have been (or perhaps could be) so designed, opportunities for job modification may need to be sought. A useful technique is to start by asking the professionals what they like to do best and what they enjoy doing least. No guarantees should be made that individuals will never have to do work they dislike, but when specialization is possible, preferences should be considered. People are likely to do what they most enjoy better and with greater satisfaction. In reference and collection development staffing, subject specialization is frequently effective and provides an additional area for continuing professional growth, as well as increasing job satisfaction. When a staff member enjoys more of a generalist work role, assignments to broad-based problems of library operations will be more effective. In addition to increasing job satisfaction, job enrichment allows the individual to feel unique or special, with a job that is not simply a carbon copy of everyone else's.

Job Modification

Job modification can include redesigning any part of the content of the job, including tasks, functions, and responsibilities, to match the individual's needs, as long as the needs of the organization are also met. If a public services librarian loves to work with the elderly and cringes each time an adolescent approaches the desk, it may be possible to have this librarian take on the responsibilities of the local genealogy files, working with the volunteers who assist the library with this service. At the same time, the librarian's public service hours could be during the regular school hours of the local junior and senior high schools, reducing the likelihood of that librarian serving a lot of adolescent patrons. Conversely, the librarian who really enjoys working with young adult patrons might be encouraged to set up a separate service location for this age group and coordinate community activities for young adults with library activities for them.

Job Rotation

Job rotation is one way to more equitably distribute the most stressful work assignments. Imagine a library in which no one wants the responsibility for equipment maintenance or service statistics. An equipment maintenance log could be developed that included descriptions of one page or less for simple maintenance problems as well as a single log for notation of what was done when. Telephone numbers, maintenance contract information, and equipment serial numbers could also be part of this single record.

Staff professionals could take the responsibility for overseeing equipment maintenance on a rotating basis, passing the logbook on every three months at a staff meeting. Service statistics could be broken down into very concrete groups collected by a variety of rotating staff members and compiled by someone else. Random samples could be utilized instead of continuous records. The collected statistics could be revised to match what is readily available from automated systems. Job rotation is already used systematically by most libraries with public service operations, which routinely give staff members turns on circulation and reference desks. If a particular period of the day is more stressful than other times, the turns covering peak times could be made shorter than those covering other periods.

Job rotation can also be used to provide equitable time for more desirable and variable professional tasks (Huff et al., 1983). For instance, staff-level library research can be encouraged by providing librarians with a rotating period of time when other routine assignments are significantly reduced, allowing an opportunity for proposal development, data collection, and writing. In school libraries, opportunities to work with teachers as media specialists in the cooperative development of new educational materials may be arranged by providing an individual school librarian with staff from elsewhere within the school system for a regular period of library coverage.

OPPORTUNITIES FOR AUTONOMY

As Chapter 2 clearly showed, there is a significant amount of research pertaining to the relationship between lack of autonomy and prevalence of burnout. Maslach (1982) puts the problem succinctly:

> Most highly motivated professionals expect to be able to do things their own way, to have a reasonable degree of control over their work environment, and to be paid enough to have independence and control over their lives outside of work. (Maslach, 1982, p. 37)

Library managers can make efforts to increase individual autonomy, but there may be some areas of concern that necessarily remain controlled in the organizational hierarchy. For example, managers can recommend and advocate librarian salaries commensurate not only with national norms but also with the graduate education required for this work, but it is unlikely that an individual manager will have the authority to set a specific salary range for all librarians. Managers can, and should, provide other areas where autonomy may be exercised, however. Professionals might be offered opportunities to schedule work hours that are not dictated by public service needs. Flextime, a system in which staff members complete a mutually agreed upon workday or workweek within certain outside parameters, such as 7:00 a.m. to 7:00 p.m. Monday through Saturday, might be used to increase staff autonomy. Professionals might also be given increased control of resources pertaining to specific jobs. For example, control of the budget areas for interlibrary loan services might be given to the interlibrary loan professional. Increased personal accountability for setting individual goals and measuring their accomplishment further enhances autonomy.

The extent to which the library administration interferes with the individual autonomy toward goal achievement should be minimized for best burnout prevention. Annoyances such as unnecessary paperwork, red tape, and excessive time delays to get administrative approval of requests should be addressed by the manager so that ways can be sought to minimize these while maintaining effective overall control of the library operations.

It is impossible, however, for every professional to act autonomously all the time. Within a bureaucratic organization, chaos would soon reign supreme. One way to increase the sense of autonomy while addressing group as well as individual needs is to utilize staff meetings to reframe individual problems into group issues and unite staff members to solve them. In numbers there is a feeling of power, and in staff meetings that are taken seriously as input for participative management, there is power. This power enhances the sense of the individual that autonomy can flourish in the environment.

POSITIVE FEEDBACK

Repeatedly, studies have shown that individuals working in large organizations crave individual recognition. Technical appreciation is particularly important. The value of a compliment offered by someone who doesn't really have a sense of what it took to achieve the result is so diluted as to make the compliment relatively meaningless. At the same time, the value of a compliment from someone who really understands the nature of the accomplishment is enhanced, making it a thrilling and prized memory of achievement. A lone library manager may not be able to single-handedly provide all the positive feedback that is needed, but the manager can do a lot to promote peer recognition by encouraging staff to pay attention to each other's good work and reinforcing lateral recognition.

Direct feedback should be timely, positive, and informative. Although it is nice to hear generalized praise at times ("Thank you; I know I can always rely on you"), more specific feedback is required to counteract the burnout phenomenon. It is recommended that managers consider having regular brief meetings, on a biweekly or monthly basis, with supervised professionals. At these meetings, the professionals have an opportunity to expand on what they are doing, how it is coming along, what problems they have encountered, and what they need to meet their goals. Managers have a splendid opportunity to provide direct feedback. Positive reinforcement ("I like that"; "You're doing a good job on this"; "That's very insightful"; "You really analyzed the problem well and your recommended solution looks like it will work") is easily provided, and most managers need little training in how to give appropriate positive comments. However, many of them have difficulty making a positive comment out of a negative observation. Here are some samples of how this might be done.

> In response to an atypical and somewhat esoteric view of the problem situation, the manager is concerned that unfeasible solutions may result and wants the staff member to go a little more with the mainstream: "That's a fascinating approach and a very unusual view of the problem. Please expand these ideas to include the typical approaches as well, so we can readily compare them."

> The library staff member has addressed only part of the problem, and some important pieces are being left out: "That certainly fits what we decided was the crux of the issue. Since then, I've been thinking that we may need to anticipate some broader issues. Let's brainstorm some of these ideas together."

> A staff librarian has a terrific goal but no inkling of the realistic cost factors that will probably shoot the project down if it isn't modified: "I like your ideas about decreasing the time it takes the patron to fill out the circulation request cards. We'll need more specific cost information on the required hardware before we can try for budget approval. Would you be willing to contact

some vendors and coordinate the information we collect? I'd also like your input on it as we go along."

The library manager has been trying unsuccessfully to get a library staff member to set accomplishable and realistic goals, as burnout potential seems quite high. The librarian has a strong tendency to overestimate personal capacities and to strive for perfection: "This project has certainly grown! I think it's time to give you an extra couple pairs of hands. It seems like it would be helpful to have someone with a lot of practical experience and someone who maybe doesn't have as much experience but is eager to be involved. Who do you think might be most helpful to you?"

The timing of positive feedback is extremely important. Recognition that comes weeks or months after completion of a laudable accomplishment has little impact. The shorter the space of time between the accomplishment and its recognition, the greater an impact that recognition will have on the staff member. When there is too long a delay between a deed and its recognition, it feels as if there was no recognition at all. Library managers must be especially cognizant of the need for positive feedback in new graduates, who are used to concrete and frequent feedback in the form of grades earned throughout and at the end of each semester. If your library's formal appraisal system does not provide a good opportunity for early interim performance review, create an informal system for yourself. All new employees, not just recent graduates, need an extra emphasis on positive feedback at first, to balance the many "don'ts" presented to them from a variety of sources while they are learning the systems and procedures of your particular library operation.

Incentive Programs

Positive feedback outside the organizational hierarchy is also an effective resource to enhance self-esteem and reduce chances of burnout. In some organizations, patrons and peers are encouraged to nominate and vote for employees of the month or year, with special "perks" accompanying the award. A priority parking space, media coverage, or a tangible form of recognition such as a plaque or service pin might be offered. However, it is very important to make the relationship between staff behavior and the incentive system very clear. A clear relationship helps reduce burnout. An unclear connection between behavior and the incentive system enhances burnout by suggesting that rewards are controlled by chance or luck rather than being related to accomplishments.

Appreciation Programs

An alternative to incentives is to increase peer support through a rotation of recognition periods. Having a variety of appreciation weeks in which staff are encouraged to provide positive feedback to those being recognized, while those being recognized are encouraged to show off a bit, may be useful. For example, a technical services appreciation week might be scheduled for March, approximately eight weeks after the introduction of a new automated serials acquisitions system. The system can be demonstrated for staff who haven't seen it, and there will have been time for some staff to appreciate what the new system can do, providing an additional impetus for identifying opportunities for positive feedback. Other appreciation programs provide recognition for the suggestions that are most cost-effective or work-efficient.

WIN-WIN ATMOSPHERE

Organizational climate can promote or inhibit the growth of burnout in the organization and is an important consideration for library managers. Litweis and Stringer (1968) define organizational climate as the measurable properties that are perceived both directly and indirectly, and that are assumed to influence the employees in terms of behavior and motivation. These properties may be explicit, as in policies and procedures, or they may be implicit in the way people within the organization interact with one another. Both explicit and implicit properties have an influence on individual staff members, who see them as defining the outside limits beyond which it is not safe to stray if one values the job and wants to keep it. Managerial attitudes, philosophies, values, and goals are reflected in the organizational climate and can effect a change in the climate when they are changed. When a library can create a win-win atmosphere in which organizational needs are served to the same positive extent that individual needs are met, burnout is likely to recede to only a remote possibility.

In many bureaucracies, the imbalance of power (a few people have control over what many more people do) creates an atmosphere of organizational gamesmanship. Through such games, efforts to equalize or redistribute power are primary and the games may take many forms. However, they all have one thing in common: There have to be at least two "players," and when one player "wins" the other "loses." If one is on the losing side too often, a high risk for burnout results. To decrease the possibility of burnout, a reduction in game playing is helpful. To really reduce the burnout potential of the library, an effort to create a permanent win-win atmosphere is recommended. Mutual goal setting, negotiation, clearly communicated needs, effectively assertive interpersonal skills, and a willingness to compromise at times are required for a win-win environment.

Participation

Potter (1980) says that "participation helps make employees burnout-resistant" (p. 183). The more influence professionals feel that they have over decisions related directly to their work, the less likely they are to experience burnout. A lack of direct input into policy decisions has been identified as a specific factor in the burnout of reference librarians (Ferriero and Powers, 1982).

Opportunities to Grow

Learning new things is one of the best ways for those who are not experiencing burnout to prevent its occurrence, as it enhances self-esteem and increases professional competence while helping the librarian maintain a mind-set of life-long learning, an attitude that is opposed to the concept of perfection as an attainable goal. However, burnout victims may not have the energy to seek out opportunities for professional growth. Their emotional resources exhausted, they may not consider themselves worthy of such opportunities or capable of deriving benefit from them. Physically exhausted, they may see the effort as too tiring. Mentally exhausted, they may find it too challenging and complex.

The library manager who is alert to burnout issues may need to provide more limited experiences along with an emphasis on support and encouragement to get the burning-out librarian to benefit from opportunities for professional growth. Arranging for more than one staff member to attend a meeting, for example, reduces the physical demands on burning-out librarians by making available group transportation and environmental assistance in finding their way around a new location. The manager may also find it beneficial to place a greater emphasis on exposure than on a specific learning goal, identifying and asserting the value of seeing the presenters in person and hearing them speak rather than simply reading their materials. The manager can also encourage professional staff members to spend time in groups with librarians from many different libraries for the pleasure of hearing a lot of different ideas expressed. If there is no requirement that new ideas be brought back to the library, the burning-out librarian need not feel increased stress, and if an idea does prove useful, the library gets a bonus in addition to a more effective staff member.

Advocacy

One of the most important functions of a manager who supervises professionals is that of advocate. The manager must see to it that the organization recognizes the skill level and needs of the staff professional, utilizing appropriate recognitions and tangible rewards for these employees, who may be as motivated by intrinsic satisfiers, such as opportunities to work on challenging new projects or personal satisfaction in professional competency, as by extrinsic motivators, such as money or vacation time. When organizational stressors promote staff burnout, it is the manager who needs to identify these to higher-level administration in order to seek to eliminate or reduce them for the benefit of the remainder of the staff.

Staff Meetings

Organizations that inhibit open communication between employees are more likely to see burnout among staff members, while organizations that encourage the open expression of feelings and the development of shared goals among peers are less likely to notice a high level of burnout victims on staff (Maslach, 1982). Staff meetings that allow free and interactive discussion can help in promoting personal expression. If the gist of such staff meetings is then used as input into organizational decision making, the effect they have on reducing burnout is even greater.

It is sometimes difficult to hold productive staff meetings when staff complaints are an agenda item. The most effective way to guide the meeting to a positive outcome for all concerned is to associate the expression of problems with the eventual outcome of recommended solutions. These may or may not occur at the same meeting, but the closer their coincidence in time, the more supported the staff will feel in regard to having their needs attended to and met. One way a manager might try to associate recommended solutions with problems is to plan a period of time for free expression of the complaints, including how people are feeling. This should be followed by a period of time in which the problem is redefined from a more cognitive analytical approach. These two steps should follow each other closely in time. The third step is to imagine as many alternative solutions to the defined problem as possible. Discussion of the different solutions is the final step, in which the expression of feelings again becomes important: The best solution is one that deals with the analytical definition of the problem without losing sight of its emotional impact on the staff or patrons. The brainstorming and solution selection steps may be separated in time from the recognition and definition steps if the problem is new or complex, or may follow immediately if the problem is chronic and the impetus of taking quick action is desired.

Daily Management

Watching the public services area of a library for unusually heavy traffic makes just as much sense as it does in a supermarket or other retail establishment. Reducing the user-to-librarian ratio makes staff members feel less pressured and better able to cope with service demand (Ferriero and Powers, 1982). But doing this only at anticipated peak times may not be enough. Keeping an eye on what's happening in public service is possible when the manager occasionally practices management-by-walking-around, which also allows the manager to respond to unusual needs when they occur. Asking another librarian to help out for ten minutes when two or three patrons are waiting their turn at a service desk is not only good sense, it is also good service. More important, it is good burnout prevention for the staff.

Encouraging the staff to take regular lunchtimes and discouraging them from putting in a lot of unpaid overtime are also important daily cares of the library manager who wishes to reduce burnout potential. Promoting variety by encouraging staff to exchange tasks as well as ideas and supporting continuing library education opportunities for all staff are also helpful.

The Physical Environment

The manager may have greater opportunity to effect changes in the physical environment than the individual librarian. By seeking to ameliorate problems of noise, pollution, and extreme temperatures, the manager can help promote an environment that contributes less to burnout. Some changes are really simple to implement, too. Repositioning of noisy equipment such as patron-operated photocopiers and change machines away from busy work areas is one idea. Rearranging large work areas so there are some open spaces rather than a sense of clutter (no matter that it is all work-related) produces less stress. Encouraging personalization of private work spaces can be complemented by attempts to create comfortable and emotionally soothing communal rest areas. Painting restroom or lounge walls in pastel colors or adding soft watercolor prints to the walls generally do not prove a great strain on the library budget. Using soft white lighting instead of regular light bulbs and ensuring adequate light for all work locations is also easily implemented. In geographic locations where significant seasonal changes occur, adjusting temperature controls and moving public service desks farther from opening outside doors may also be helpful.

EMPLOYEE HEALTH PROGRAMS

Libraries have not paid as much attention to the possibility of employee health and fitness programs as many other businesses have. Patrick (1984a) reports that businesses that have implemented these programs have experienced benefits such as decreased absenteeism, fewer work-related accidents, more effective coping with workplace stress, and increased positive work attitudes. Employee fitness programs take some thought, as they need to be safe as well as provide a variety of options. A program that promotes one "right way" denies individual differences and is not as effective in combating burnout.

Programs may vary from providing on-site equipment, sometimes in staffed environments, to providing premiums or discounts for health club memberships. Didactic training may be offered, such as talks on smoking cessation, weight reduction, or stress management. Recreational activities may be promoted by library sponsorship of employee teams for softball or volleyball, or by encouraging employees to informally engage in these activities. Some programs require minimal managerial effort at all, for example, encouraging staff (and perhaps accompanying them) to do "stack walking" similar to the popular suburban practice of mall walking in inclement weather. Some efforts require significant levels of administrative support, as in large organizations where psychological counseling services may be offered. Although on-site services may be beyond the resources of many libraries, professional assistance can be very effective in treating burnout victims before they become either deadwood or career jumpers. The manager can assist staff by supporting and encouraging those who feel a need for this assistance, and perhaps by maintaining a resource file of agencies where burnout counseling is available. Confidentiality must, of course, be very strictly respected when staff members approach their manager on this issue.

Development of physical and emotional strength in advance of unusual drains on these personal resources is the theory of wellness programs that are planned to reduce burnout potential in high-stress occupations. For most people, however, health and fitness programs have to be fun to keep them coming back for more. They also have to be relatively accessible, as people are more likely to go to them if it is not difficult to do so. They need to be safe, as injuries or unanticipated medical complications are clearly undesirable.

SUPPORT AND MENTORING

Throughout the literature on burnout, the concept of emotional support is brought up again and again. Support is a means by which people are made to feel that management is on their side. To be supportive, the manager must believe that people have the right to make their own decisions and take responsibility for the consequences of those decisions. The manager's role is to provide them with some additional strength to do so. Individual support can be provided by family and friends and by peers, but should also be provided by supervisors. The library manager may also play a role in promoting peer support within the library.

Supervisory Support

Supervisors can support burnout victims by making sure effective stress management techniques and coping strategies can be practiced in the library environment. For instance, providing a place to spend breaks and encouraging the use of these rest breaks are important. Listening empathetically and offering advice when it is solicited may also be part of the supervisor's role. Confidentiality is an important issue when providing support, and supervisors must remember that even a minor breach of confidentiality can erode the entire trust within the supervisory relationship, making them impotent to help.

Peer Support

Library managers can encourage active staff discussion on issues that are controversial or pressure-generating. Letting staff know that they are not facing issues alone is important. In a group setting, the manager can watch for ways to point out similarities of experiences and feelings and to reinforce productive coping strategies.

Mentoring

Maslow (1954) long ago suggested that the pinnacle of human motivation, after lower-order needs were met, was striving for self-actualization. Not every job has opportunities for growth to self-actualization, and not all professionals seek this level in their work. Yet, for many of them, professional growth is an integral part of their ideal, fully actualized self. In organizations with high burnout potential, there is little opportunity for this level of growth. Mentoring may be one way an individual manager can provide such opportunities. True mentoring is a process whereby an established professional systematically provides learning experiences and work opportunities to less established professionals in order to promote their professional growth and development. In a good mentoring relationship, the mentor guides the neophyte along until the mentor's own level of skill and expertise is reached. At this point, mentors need to be willing to assist their newly established peers in finding jobs similar to the mentors' own, or in replacing the mentors if they choose to vacate their own positions.

If neither additional opportunity arises, good mentors work cooperatively within the organizational system, continuing to provide support.

SUMMARY

The library manager can play an important role in reducing the amount of burnout promoted by the work environment and in increasing opportunities for effective stress management in the library. Establishing and maintaining realistic goals and expectations is one way managers can help reduce chronic work-related stressors. An emphasis on providing opportunities for professional autonomy and giving positive feedback within a framework of clearly identified lines of authority and responsibility also helps the manager create a less stressful work environment for staff. Perhaps most important, the manager can help provide and maintain an organizational climate that promotes win-win interactions rather than win-lose conflicts or no-win traps. Of course, any systematic organizational intervention to prevent, reduce, or reverse burnout requires the commitment of top administration and effective, understanding middle managers.

Chapter 8
Finale

The best advice that can be given to someone who is in danger of burning out can be summed up in a single contracted word: DON'T. Burnout is an incredibly uncomfortable and distressing state of total exhaustion, including emotional exhaustion, physical exhaustion, and mental exhaustion. Chronic work-related stress experienced over long periods becomes overwhelming, and effective everyday functioning is seriously compromised. Fortunately, burnout is preventable. It is also stoppable and reversible if you are already experiencing it. There is hope.

This book has tried to present an overview of what burnout is, how you can recognize it, and what you can do about it. It is meant to be optimistic. Librarianship is a satisfying and fulfilling career that can bring joy into your life. As a helping profession in a complex technological world of information explosion and a society of high stress, librarianship can be risky in terms of potential burnout. But knowledge is power, and by knowing what you risk, you can overcome it.

FINAL REVIEW

Burnout is a total experience of chronic work-related stresses resulting in emotional, physical, and mental exhaustion that has been recognized for a little more than a decade. It was first recognized in social workers dealing with recipients of community services. Specific work-related stressors have been highly correlated with the process of burnout through a number of empirical studies. These include a lack of professional autonomy (librarians have little authority over what they do on a daily basis); dealing with the public in a demanding and highly variable role; role conflicts of many types (these may be as simple as a mismatch between you and the job or as complex as a mismatch between the job requirements and your personal values); role ambiguity (where what you are supposed to do is exceedingly unclear); a decreased sense of personal accomplishment; inadequate positive feedback; lack of control over work operations; no-win situations; and continuously heavy workloads. Some library-specific stressors have also been reported by librarians as chronic problems contributing to their experience of burnout. These include, among others, dealing with censorship issues and fighting the library stereotype.

If you are idealistic, committed to your profession, single-minded, and perfectionistic, your potential for burnout is likely to be high. It may also be increased if you are single, childless, and young.

A myriad of signs and symptoms of burnout exist, conveniently categorized into three groups: emotional, physical, and behavioral. All of the signs and symptoms of burnout occur in the everyday lives of most people. In the burnout process they start out being specifically related to work activities and gradually generalize to make your whole life miserable. You may feel isolated and incompetent, experience numerous negative emotions, have interpersonal conflicts, get sick, become intellectually duller, and demonstrate deteriorating work performance.

A variety of helping professionals have been found to be susceptible to burnout. Among them are mental health workers, nurses, attorneys, police officers, members of the clergy, and librarians. Research studies produced by librarians about librarians have shown that reference librarians, school librarians, and special librarians seem particularly at risk. Library managers estimate that the majority of their staff professionals have experienced burnout.

Burnout occurs as a process of several stages, and librarians go through it in ways similar to people in other helping professions. Initially, enthusiasm is exceptionally high and is coupled with unrealistic expectations that can be shattered by reality. A period of competence is concurrent with a period of stagnation, as the professional continues to strive for unreachable goals against odds of limited resources and limited power. Frustration sets in, with primary feelings of depression, followed by an apathy stage. However, intervention is possible at any or all stages to reduce the impact of burnout, to stop its progression, and to reverse it.

You can find out whether you are a candidate for burnout (or an incumbent) by self-monitoring and by obtaining feedback from people who know you well, both inside and outside the workplace. You can anticipate work environments that promote or enhance the burnout process. Specific tools to help you with this are the PBQ (Personal Burnout Quotient) and the JBQ (Job Burnout Quotient), which were devised specifically for librarians.

Individually, you can practice effective stress management to help you in preventing or reversing burnout as necessary. From relaxation techniques to hobbies, thousands of coping strategies are available to help you on a personal level with managing stress and burnout. Only a few of these many possible coping strategies have been suggested here, but they were selected carefully as those most likely to prove effective for most people.

Your library can also help you prevent burnout if you have management that is interested and knowledgeable. Modifying jobs, clarifying authority and responsibility, creating a win-win atmosphere, establishing and maintaining realistic job expectations, providing opportunities for autonomy, and giving positive feedback are all ways your library management can ensure preservation of their most valuable resource: you.

LAST WORDS

Burnout is not an ending, but a beginning. It gives you an opportunity to get to know yourself better, to refresh yourself, and to make your life much more enjoyable and comfortable. Stress is not always harmful, it is inevitable, and it can be helpful. Burnout is harmful and is neither inevitable nor helpful unless you use it to improve your life. To achieve your personal goal of avoiding or treating burnout, you must learn to put stress in perspective and manage it wisely.

You can do this. And you are not alone.

References

Argyris, C. (1957). *Personality and organization.* New York: Harper & Row.

Argyris, C. (1964). *Integrating the individual and the organization.* New York: Wiley.

Armstrong, K. L. (1978). How can we avoid burnout? In M. L. Lauderdale, K. N. Anderson, and S. E. Cramer (eds.), *Child abuse and neglect: Issues on innovation and implementation. Vol. 2. Proceedings of the 2nd Annual National Conference on Child Abuse and Neglect,* April 17–20, 1977. DHEW Publication (OHDS) No. 78-30148 (pp. 230–238). Washington, DC: USGPO.

Beehr, T. A., and Newman, J. E. (1978). Job stress, employee health and organizational effectiveness: A facet analysis, model and literature review. *Personnel Journal, 31,* 655–699.

Benson, H. (1975). *The relaxation response.* New York: William Morrow.

Bitcon, C. H. (1981). Guest editorial: Professional burnout. *Journal of Music Therapy, 18*(1), 2–6.

Bly, L. (1981). Burn-out. *Arkansas Libraries, 38,* September, 24.

Bold, R. (1982). Librarian burn-out. *Library Journal, 107,* 2048–2051.

Brill, P. L. (1984). The need for an operational definition of burnout. *Family and Community Health, 6*(4), 12–24.

Bunge, C. A. (1984). Potential and reality at the reference desk: Reflections on a "return to the field." *Journal of Academic Librarianship, 10*(3), 128–132.

Bunge, C. A. (1987). Stress in the library. *Library Journal, 112*(15), 47–51.

Caplan, G. (1964). *Principles of preventive psychiatry.* New York: Basic Books.

Caputo, J. S. (1984). *The assertive librarian.* Phoenix, AZ: Oryx Press.

Carrilio, T. E., and Eisenberg, D. M. (1984). Using peer support to prevent worker burnout. *Social Casework, 65*(5), 307–310.

Cherniss, C. (1980). *Professional burnout in human services organizations.* New York: Praeger.

Cherniss, C. (1982). Cultural trends: Political, economic, and historical roots of the problem. In W. S. Paine (ed.), *Job stress and burnout: Research, theory, and intervention perspectives* (pp. 83–94). Beverly Hills, CA: Sage.

Cherry, L. (1978). On the real benefits of eustress (Hans Selye interview). *Psychology Today,* March, 60–64.

Cooper, C. L. (1973). *Group training for organizational development.* Basel, Switzerland: Karger.

Cooper, C. L., and Marshall, J. (1976). Occupational sources of stress. *Journal of Occupational Psychology, 49,* 11–28.

Coping with stress. (1980). *Unabashed Librarian, 37,* 9.

Daniels, L. A. (1985). How to understand and control stress. *Hospital Topics, 63*(4), 12–15, 21, 48.

Dworkin, A. G. (1987). *Teacher burnout in the public schools: Structural causes and consequences for children.* Albany, NY: State University of New York Press.

Edelwich, J., and Brodsky, A. (1980). *Burnout: Stages of disillusionment in the helping professions.* New York: Human Sciences Press.

Elliott, J. L., and Smith, N. M. (1984). Burnout. *School Library Media Quarterly, 12*(2), 136, 141–145.

Etzion, D., and Pines, A. (1981). Sex and culture as factors explaining burnout and coping among human service professionals: A social psychological perspective. *Journal of Cross Cultural Psychology, 17*(2), 191–209.

Ferriero, D. S., and Powers, K. A. (1982). Burnout at the reference desk. *RQ, 21*(3), 274–279.

Fox, A. (1980). Burnout . . . really hit home. *American Journal of Nursing, 80,* 226.

French, J. R. P., and Caplan, R. D. (1972). Organizational stress and individual strain. In D. W. Organ (ed.), *The applied psychology of work behavior.* Dallas, TX: Business Publications, Inc.

Freudenberger, H. (1974). Staff burn-out. *Journal of Social Issues, 30,* 159–165.

Freudenberger, H. (1977). Burn-out: The organizational menace. *Training and Development Journal,* July, 26–27.

Freudenberger, H., and Richelson, G. (1980). *Burn-out: The high cost of high achievement.* Garden City, NY: Anchor.

Glicken, M. D. (1983). A counseling approach to employee burnout. *Personnel Journal, 62*(3), 222–228.

Goldberger, L., and Breznitz, S. (eds.) (1982). *Handbook of stress: Theoretical and clinical aspects.* New York: Macmillan, Free Press.

Gray-Toft, P. (1980). Effectiveness of a counseling support program for hospice nurses. *Journal of Counseling Psychology, 27,* 346–354.

Haack, M., Jones, J. W., and Roose, T. (1984). Occupational burnout among librarians. *Drexel Library Quarterly, 20,* 46–72.

Harris, P. L. (1984). Assessing burnout: The organizational and individual perspective. *Family and Community Health, 6*(4), 32–43.

Helliwell, T. (1981). Are you a potential burnout? *Training and Development Journal, 35*(10), 25–29.

Hendrickson, B. (1979). Teachers combat burnout. *Learning, 7,* b.

Huff, M. R., Williams L., Crothers, R. W., Driver, P. S., Endo, R. K., Manske, T. A., and Sasich, L. (1983). Preventing burnout: An alternative approach. *Hospital Pharmacy, 18,* 588–589.

Jones, J. (1981). Staff burnout and employee counterproductivity. In J. Jones (ed.), *The burnout syndrome* (pp. 126–138). Park Ridge, IL: London House Press.

Justice, B., Gold, R. S., and Klein, J. P. (1981). Life events and burnout. *Journal of Psychology, 108,* 219–226.

Justice, B., and Justice, R. (1981). *The complete book of stress and creative coping.* Houston, TX: Peak Press.

Kahn, R., Wolfe, D., Quinn, R., Snoek, J., and Rosenthal, R. A. (1964). *Organizational stress: Studies in role conflict and ambiguity.* New York: Wiley.

Kermish, I., and Kushin, F. (1969). Why high turnover? Social staff losses in a county welfare agency. *Public Welfare, 27,* 34–35.

Lazarus, A. (1979). Positive denial: The case for not facing reality. *Psychology Today,* November, 1979.

Leighton, S. L., and Roye, A. K. (1984). Prevention and self-care for professional burnout. *Family and Community Health, 6*(4), 44–56.

Litweis, G. H., and Stringer, R. A., Jr. (1968). *Motivation and original climate.* Cambridge, MA: Harvard University Press.

Loomba, M. (1982). Burnout and the college librarian: A view from Westchester. In C. A. Burns (ed.), *Insight, 1981–82: An annual collection of articles on teaching and learning by faculty of the Community Colleges of the State University of New York* (pp. 12–19). Albany, NY: State University of New York Press.

Maher, E. L. (1983). Burnout and commitment: A theoretical alternative. *Personnel and Guidance Journal, 61,* 390–393.

Maslach, C. (1982). *Burnout: The cost of caring.* New York: Prentice-Hall.

Maslach, C., and Jackson, S. E. (1978). Lawyer burnout. *Barister, 8,* 52–58.

Maslach, C., and Jackson, S. E. (1979). Burned out cops and their families. *Psychology Today,* December, 59–62.

Maslach, C., and Jackson, S. E. (1981). The Maslach Burnout Inventory. Palo Alto, CA: Consulting Psychologists Press.

Maslach, C., and Pines, A. (1977). The burn-out syndrome in the day care setting. *Child Care Quarterly, 6,* 100–113.

Maslach, C., and Pines, A. (1979). Burnout: The loss of human caring. In A. Pines and C. Maslach (eds.), *Experiencing social psychology* (pp. 246–252). New York: Knopf.

Maslow, A. H. (1954). *Motivation and personality.* New York: Harper and Row.

Matteson, M. T., and Ivancevich, J. M. (1982). The how, what and why of stress management training. *Personnel Journal, 61,* 768–774.

McQuade, W., and Aikman, A. (1974). *Stress.* New York: Bantam.

Melendez, W. A., and Guzman, R. M. (1983). *Burnout: The new academic disease* (ASHE-ERIC Education Report Series, No. 9). Washington, DC: Association for the Study of Higher Education.

Minnehan, R. F., and Paine, W. S. (1982). Bottom lines, Assessing the economic and legal consequences of burnout. In W. S. Paine (ed.), *Job stress and burnout: Research, theory, and intervention perspectives* (pp. 95–112). Beverly Hills, CA: Sage.

Morrow, T. (1981). The burnout of almost everybody. *Time,* September 21, p. 84.

Morse, D. R., and Furst, M. L. (1982). *Women under stress.* New York: Van Nostrand Reinhold.

Mueller, R. K. (1979). *Career conflict.* Cambridge, MA: Arthur D. Little.

Muldary, T. (1983). *Burnout and health professionals: Manifestations and management.* New York: Appleton & Lange.

Neville, S. H. (1981). Job stress and burnout: Occupational hazards for services staff. *College and Research Libraries, 42,* 242–247.

Paine, W. S. (ed.) (1982). *Job stress and burnout: Research, theory, and intervention perspectives.* Beverly Hills, CA: Sage.

Paine, W. S. (1984). Professional burnout: Some major costs. *Family and Community Health, 6*(4), 1–11.

Patrick, P. K. S. (1979). Burnout: Job hazard for health workers. *Hospitals,* November, 87–89.

Patrick, P. K. (1984a). Organizational strategies: Promoting retention and job satisfaction. *Family and Community Health, 6*(4), 57–67.

Patrick, P. K. (1984b). Professional roles at risk for burnout. *Family and Community Health, 6*(4), 25–31.

Payette, M., and Guay, E. (1981). Le stress: Comment certains bibliothecaires le vivent. *Argus, 10,* 121–127.

Pearse, R., and Peizer, P. (1975). *Self-directed change for the mid career manager.* New York: AMACOM.

Pennebaker, J. W. (1982). *The psychology of physical symptoms.* New York: Springer-Verlag.

Perlman, B., and Hartman, E. A. (1982). Burnout: Summary and future research. *Human Relations, 35,* 283–305.

Pfifferling, J. H., and Eckel, F. M. (1982). Beyond burnout: Obstacles and prospects. In W. S. Paine (ed.), *Job stress and burnout: Research, theory, and intervention perspectives* (pp. 257–265). Beverly Hills, CA: Sage.

Pines, A. (1981a). Helper's motivation and the burnout syndrome. In T. A. Wells (ed.), *Basic processes in helping relationships.* New York: Academic Press.

Pines, A. (1981b). A current problem in pediatrics. *Current Problems in Pediatrics,* May, pp. 1–46.

Pines, A. M. (1982). Changing organizations: Is a work environment without burnout an impossible goal? In W. S. Paine (ed.), *Job stress and burnout: Research, theory, and intervention perspectives* (pp. 189–211). Beverly Hills, CA: Sage.

Pines, A., and Aronson, E. (1980). Burnout: From tedium to personal growth. Paper presented at the meeting of the American Psychological Association, Montreal, September.

Pines, A., and Aronson, E. (1981). *Burnout: From tedium to personal growth.* New York: Macmillan, Free Press.

Pines, A., and Aronson, E. (1988). *Career burnout: Causes and cures.* New York: Macmillan, Free Press.

Pines, A., Aronson, E., and Kafry, D. (1981). *Burnout: From tedium to personal growth.* New York: Macmillan, Free Press.

Pines, A., and Kanner, A. (1982). Nurses burnout: Lack of positive conditions and presence of negative conditions as two independent sources of stress. In E. A. McConnell (ed.), *Burnout in the nursing profession.* St. Louis, MO: Mosby.

Pines, A., and Maslach, C. (1978). Characteristics of staff burnout in mental health settings. *Hospital and Community Psychiatry, 29,* 233–237.

Pines, A., and Maslach, C. (1980). Combatting staff burnout in a child-care center: A case study. *Child Care Quarterly, 9,* 5–16.

Plate, K., and Stone, E. W. (1976). Factors affecting librarians' job satisfaction. In R. Shimmon (ed.), *A reader in library management* (pp. 146–160). Hamden, CT: Linnet Books.

Podell, L. (1967). Attrition of first line social service staff. *Welfare Review, 5,* 9–14.

Potter, B. A. (1980). *Beating job burnout: How to transform work pressure into productivity.* San Francisco, CA: Harbor.

Potter, B. A. (1987). *Preventing job burnout.* Los Altos, CA: Crisp.

Preslan, B. (1979). Bailing out. *Library Journal, 104,* 2165–2167.

Rader, M. H. (1981). Dealing with information overload. *Personnel Journal, 60,* 373–375.

Reed, S. (1979). Teacher burnout a growing hazard. *New York Times, Educational Supplement,* January 7.

Rettig, J. (1986). The crisis in academic reference work. In B. Katz (compiler), *Reference and information services: A reader for today.* Metuchen, NJ: Scarecrow.

Richardson, M., and West, P. (1982). Motivational management: Coping with burnout. *Hospital and Community Psychiatry, 33,* 837–840.

Rooks, D. C. (1988). *Motivating today's library staff: A management guide.* Phoenix, AZ: Oryx Press.

Rosenthal, D., Teague, M., Retish, P., West, J., and Vessell, R. (1983). The relationship between work environment attributes and burnout. *Journal of Leisure Research, 15,* 125–135.

Selye, H. (1936). A syndrome produced by diverse nocuous agents. *Nature, 138,* 32.

Selye, H. (1956). *The stress of life.* New York: McGraw-Hill.

Shapiro, C. H. (1982). Creative supervision: An underutilized antidote. In W. S. Paine (ed.), *Job stress and burnout: Research, theory, and intervention perspectives* (pp. 213–228). Beverly Hills, CA: Sage.

Simendinger, E. A., and Moore, T. F. (1985). *Organizational burnout in health care facilities.* Rockville, MD: Aspen.

Smith, N. M., Birch, N. E., and Marchant, M. P. (1986). Stress, distress, and burnout: A survey of public reference librarians. *Public Libraries,* Fall, 83–85.

Smith, N. M., and Nielsen, L. F. (1984). Burnout: A survey of corporate librarians. *Special Libraries, 75,* 221–227.

Smith, N. M., and Nelson, V. C. (1983a). Burnout: A survey of academic reference librarians. *College and Research Libraries, 44,* 245–250.

Smith, N. M., and Nelson, V. C. (1983b). Helping may be harmful: The implications of burnout for the special librarian. *Special Libraries, 74,* 14–19.

Smith, N. M., and Wuehler, A. (1986). Burnout and social interest in librarians and library school students. In V. S. Hafield (ed.), *Preparing for the 21st century: Proceedings of the Mountain Plains Library Association Academic Library Section Research Forum*, Silver Creek, Colorado, October 11–15 (ERIC Document Reproduction Service No. ED 290 493).

Sorenson, R. J. (1981). Fright, flight or fight—how are you reacting to stress? *Indiana Media Journal, 3,* 3–4.

Stevens, M. J., and Pfost, K. S. (1983). A problem solving approach to staff burnout in rehabilitation settings. *Rehabilitation Counseling Bulletin, 27,* 101–107.

Sullivan, P. (1982). Belligerence. *Illinois Libraries, 64,* 1147–1148.

Taler, I. (1984). Burnout: A survey of library directors' views (ERIC Document Reproduction Service No. ED 283 524).

Tanner, L. A. (1983). Middle management stress: Recognizing and treating burnout victims. *Health Financial Management, 37,* 12–14, 18–22.

Todaro, J. B. (1982). Job burnout: It's time we had a telethon. *Illinois Libraries, 64,* 1153–1157.

Tubesing, N. L., and Tubesing, D. A. (1982). The treatment of choice: Selecting stress skills to suit the individual and the situation. In W. S. Paine (ed.), *Job stress and burnout: Research, theory, and intervention perspectives* (pp. 155–171). Beverly Hills, CA: Sage.

Veninga, R. (1979). Administrator burnout: Causes and cures. *Hospital Progress, 6*(2), 45–52.

Veninga, R. L., and Spradley, J. P. (1981). *The work stress connection: How to cope with job burnout.* Boston: Little, Brown.

Vessell, R. (1980). The devastating costs of professional burnout. *Therapeutic Recreation Journal, 14*(3), 11–14.

Visotsky, H., and Cramer, K. D. (1982). Experts cite elements of identifying, managing stress [interview]. *Hospital Employee Health, 1,* 138–140.

Walsh, D. (1979). Classroom stress and teacher burnout. *Phi Delta Kappan, 61,* 45–62.

Walsh, J. A. (1982). Burnout: The brothers grim. *Illinois Libraries, 64,* 1149–1153.

Watstein, S. B. (1979). Burnout: From a librarian's perspective (ERIC Document Reproduction Service No. ED 195 232).

Webster's ninth new collegiate dictionary (1987). Springfield, MA: Merriam-Webster Inc.

Webster's third new international dictionary of the English language, unabridged (1976). Chicago, IL: Encyclopedia Britannica.

Weinberger, P. (1970). *Job satisfaction and staff retention in social work.* San Diego, CA: San Diego State College, School of Social Work.

Wilder, J. F., and Plutchik, R. (1982). Preparing the professional: Building prevention into training. In W. S. Paine (ed.), *Job stress and burnout; Research, theory, and intervention perspectives* (pp. 113–129). Beverly Hills, CA: Sage.

Woodman, M. (1980). *The owl was a baker's daughter.* Toronto: Inner City Books.

Zastrow, C. (1984). Understanding and preventing burn-out. *British Journal of Social Work, 14,* 141–155.

Index

Compiled by Ty Koontz

JANETTE S. CAPUTO

Jan Caputo is both a librarian and clinical psychologist. As a librarian, she spent 14 years in academic and special libraries, holding management positions for 11 of those years. As a psychologist, she specializes in rehabilitation neuropsychology and is currently on the staff of Mary Free Bed Hospital and Rehabilitation Center in Grand Rapids, Michigan. Dr. Caputo's MSLS is from Wayne State University where she also earned her PhD in instructional technology. She earned her MA and PsyD in clinical psychology from Central Michigan University. She is also an accomplished violist who plays with a variety of community and semi-professional orchestras. She lives in Alma, Michigan, where she and her husband are restoring an 1880's farmhouse.